God's Secret

Notes

A Primer with Pictures for How to Rightly Divide the Word of Truth

Notes

God's Secret

Faith is believing what God says in His word.

Introduction

Hid in God from before the foundation of the earth was a SECRET that no one knew until it was "due time" to reveal it. This book is a panoramic overview of God's progressive revelation to man through His Word, the Bible. It is filled with verses from the King James Bible and pictures to help demonstrate God's dealings with all mankind, in the past, present, and future.

This book is organized in a simple way to help the reader "rightly divide the word of truth" (2 Timothy 2:15). The main division in the Bible is between "mystery" and "prophecy." When studying the Bible, it is important to be both <u>biblical</u> and <u>dispensational</u>, to know not only <u>what</u> God is saying, but to know to <u>whom, when,</u> and in <u>what context He is speaking</u>, for God has given different instructions at different times to different people.

<u>God's great wisdom in the long war against Satan is the major theme of this book.</u> His brilliant military strategy was that He kept a SECRET. God used His Son as the strategic weapon by which He won back both heaven and earth from His adversary, Satan. Other themes include Israel to be a CHANNEL OF BLESSING to the Gentiles, the distinctive ministry of the Apostle Paul, and the kingdom of God.

The Lord Jesus Christ is the Hero of His-story as revealed in the Holy Scriptures by His spokesmen. He rescued all believers by His loving sacrifice.

No other book is as exciting as the Bible. In it, we learn God's plan and purpose – what He has done, is doing, and will do. If we really want to know what is going on, it is more important to consult the Bible than the newspaper. Because there is power in God's Word, many verses from the KJB are quoted. This book is a "primer" to assist the reader in understanding the Bible better as a whole.

The goal is for "all men to be saved, and to come unto the knowledge of the truth" (1 Timothy 2:4). The book is also designed to be a tool for the members of the body of Christ to share right division with their loved ones "to make all *men* see what *is* the fellowship of the mystery" (Ephesians 3:9). Are you ready to discover the mystery of God's SECRET? ". . . the revelation of the MYSTERY, which was kept SECRET since the world began" (Rom. 16:25).

A Primer with Pictures for How to Rightly Divide the Word of Truth

Foreword

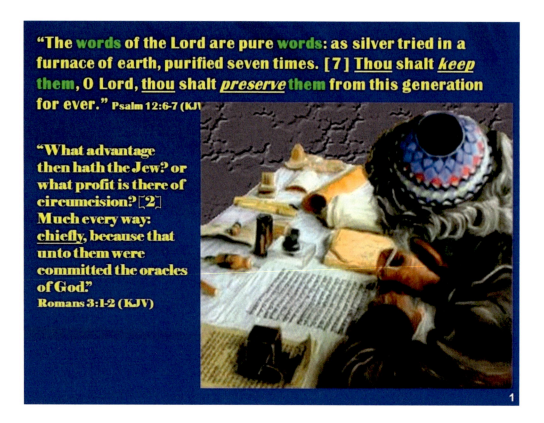

As He promised God has preserved His word. In English it is found in the King James Bible "as silver tried in a furnace of earth, purified seven times" (Psalms 12:6, 7, see above). The line of Bibles to the perfection of the KJB:

1. Tyndale - 1526

2. Coverdale - 1535

3. Matthews - 1537

4. The Great Bible - 1539

5. Geneva - 1560

6. Bishops' - 1568

7. King James – 1611

See <u>Why I Use the King James Bible</u>, in the Appendix, page 103.

God's Secret

I consider myself very blessed to have come to understand the King James Bible rightly divided (this truth is hidden in the modern bibles). My main interest when reading the Bible has always been "what is God saying?" or "for what saith the scriptures?" We need to know what God's plan is:

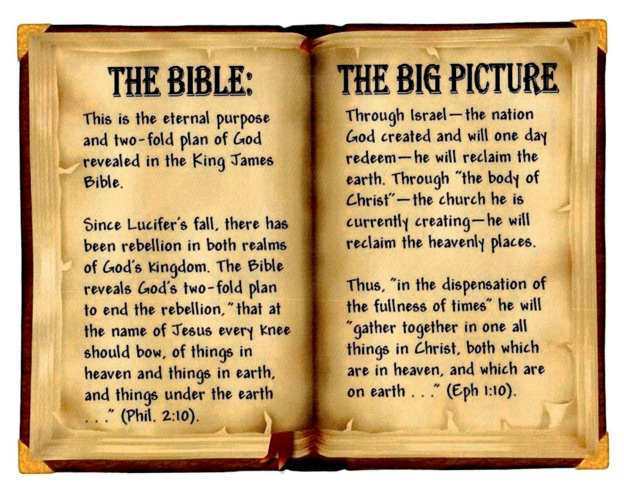

THE BIBLE: THE BIG PICTURE

This is the eternal purpose and two-fold plan of God revealed in the King James Bible.

Since Lucifer's fall, there has been rebellion in both realms of God's kingdom. The Bible reveals God's two-fold plan to end the rebellion, "that at the name of Jesus every knee should bow, of things in heaven and things in earth, and things under the earth . . ." (Phil. 2:10).

Through Israel—the nation God created and will one day redeem—he will reclaim the earth. Through "the body of Christ"—the church he is currently creating—he will reclaim the heavenly places.

Thus, "in the dispensation of the fullness of times" he will "gather together in one all things in Christ, both which are in heaven, and which are on earth . . ." (Eph 1:10).

This book is "laid out" RIGHTLY DIVIDED, into three main sections: PAST, PRESENT, and FUTURE. My hope is that people will see the "big picture" of what God has done, is doing, and will do. He so precisely, wisely, and concisely reveals this in His word, the Bible.

In God are hid: ". . . all the treasures of wisdom and knowledge" (Col. 2:3).

By reading and studying His word we can learn more about Christ. Paul wrote, "That I may know him . . ." (Phil. 3:10).

We can go on a treasure hunt in the Bible, to not only know more about our Lord Jesus Christ, but also God's plan and purpose for mankind.

A Primer with Pictures for How to Rightly Divide the Word of Truth

Romans thru Philemon = TO the Body of Christ
The remainder of our Bible = TO the Nation of Israel

Israel & Body of Christ: God's two different agencies on two different programs, with two different purposes.

I used to be a mixer. Unknowingly, I mixed the things that belonged to the nation of Israel with the things that belong to the body of Christ. I did not know that Gentiles are saved in a different way today than they were in the past. When we mix law and grace we end up with false doctrine.

God's Secret

But then I discovered that all the Bible is written "for" our learning, but not all the Bible is written "to" or "about us." I noticed that there was more than one gospel and more than one church in the Bible. I learned that I was not part of spiritual Israel. <u>This was an "aha moment."</u> I learned that God had a SECRET that He had kept hidden in Himself that He revealed in "due time" to the Apostle Paul.

In the PAST and FUTURE, God talks about His prophetic plan for Israel and other kingdom on earth believers who will be part of His Kingdom on Earth.

But in the PRESENT God has revealed the mystery that He is calling out a people to inhabit "his heavenly kingdom" (2 Tim. 4:18).

A Primer with Pictures for How to Rightly Divide the Word of Truth

I have discovered that the Bible must be rightly divided to be understood. I hope this brief overview of the Bible with pictures and verses will help you to come to the same conclusion.

I found out that the Bible says different things to different people at different times. The key is that the Bible must be rightly divided. Rightly dividing the truth does not mean to divide truth from error, it means to divide truth from truth. All the Bible is truth, but not all the Bible is our truth. Most of the Bible is to Israel and the kingdom on earth believers, while only a small portion of the Bible is directly to the body of Christ, the heavenly kingdom believers.

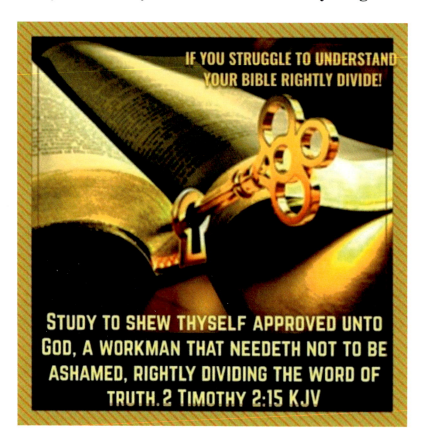

"Study to shew thyself approved unto God, a workman that needeth not to be ashamed, rightly dividing the word of truth" (2 Timothy 2:15).

We are commanded to "study" the word of God so that we may be approved to Him, and NOT be ashamed at the Judgment seat of Christ (1 Cor. 3:12-14). We are to divide truth. All the Bible is truth. No one understands all of the Bible but as we study, our spiritual understanding widens and deepens. The more we study God's Word, the more we see what we didn't see before.

God's Secret

We are living in the present, also called "But Now." It is important to know where we are.

You are here:

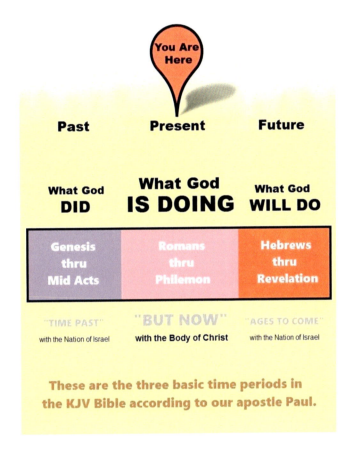

The Bible can be pictured in the following ways:
PAST – PRESENT – FUTURE
Time Past – But Now – Ages to Come
Prophecy – Mystery – Prophecy
Earth Kingdom believers–Heaven Kingdom believers–Earth Kingdom believers
Old Covenant (Law) – Grace – New Covenant (Law)
Israel, Israel, Israel, Israel, (body of Christ) Israel, Israel, Israel, Israel

_____(body of Christ)_____

If we take the parenthesis out of a sentence, what are we still left with?
A complete sentence.
_____.

A Primer with Pictures for How to Rightly Divide the Word of Truth

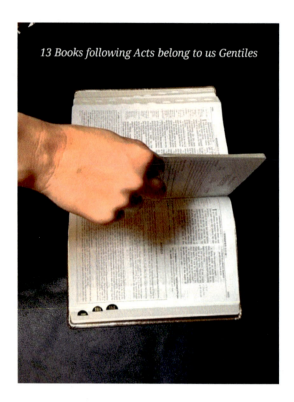

About 7% of the Bible is "to us" while the rest of the Bible is "for us." If we remove Paul's letters (Romans to Philemon) from the Bible, we essentially remove the Church, the body of Christ, from the Bible. Most of the Bible is written to and about the nation of Israel, not us. Confusion ends when we learn God's plan for heaven and earth.

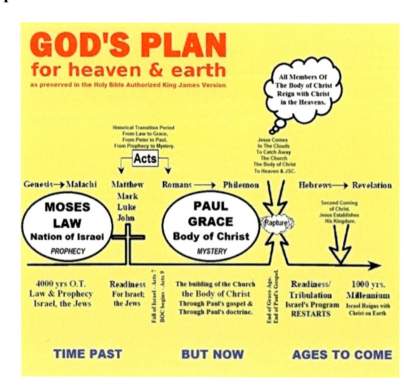

God's Secret

"You can only believe as much as you have understood" Cornelius R. Stam.

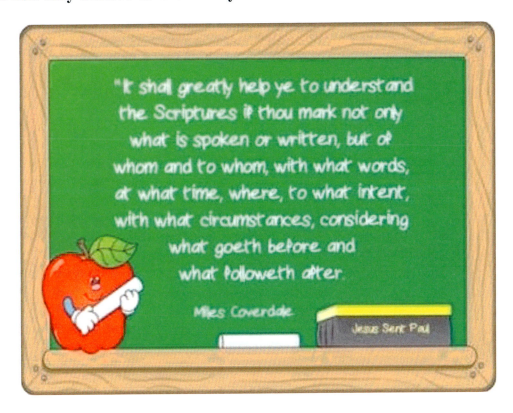

When we read the Bible it is best to take the <u>literal meaning</u> for the most part and to ask: what is written, who is speaking, to whom, when, why, and what is the prevailing circumstance (context).

A Primer with Pictures for How to Rightly Divide the Word of Truth

How to Rightly Divide the Word of Truth

There is a divinely inspired timeline embedded in the Bible which follows the order of the books of the Bible, Genesis to Mid Acts, Romans to Philemon, Hebrews to Revelation (the Dispensation of Grace began in Acts 9).

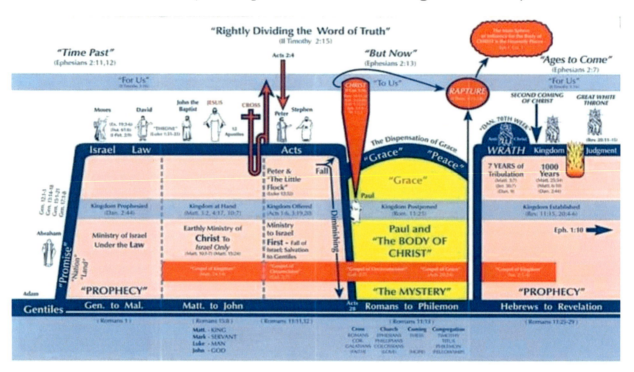

Spiritual growth can only happen after people are saved. "But the natural man receiveth not the things of the Spirit of God" (1 Cor. 2:14). To get the most out of the Bible we must also believe that God has inspired and preserved His word for us, "the word of God, which effectually worketh also in you that BELIEVE" (1 Thess. 2:13). After salvation, NOT rightly dividing can severely hurt one's spiritual growth. Because with right division we have a clear understanding of how to be saved, and what God's purpose and plan is.

Our specific instruction, <u>sound doctrine</u>, in this age of God's grace is only found in Paul's epistles, Romans through Philemon. We need to be stabilized in the truth. As you read this book, to help you understand God's plan (and purpose) for mankind, you will notice that God has an adversary, Satan, who has tried to destroy His plan. There is a battle going on between God and Satan, but he is a defeated enemy. Christ defeated Satan on the cross. Soon after that God revealed His "SECRET" to us through Paul. My desire for you is the same as Paul's ". . . that ye might be filled with the knowledge of his will in all wisdom and spiritual understanding" (Col. 1:9).

God's Secret

The Most Important Thing in Life

The most important thing in life is not fame, fortune, or happiness. No, the most important thing in life is where we spend eternity, and we only have this lifetime to decide where that will be. "And as it is appointed unto men once to die, but after this the judgment" (Heb. 9:27).

We all do wrong things because we are imperfect. God is Holy and nothing imperfect can stand before Him. We cannot clean ourselves up and be perfect.

Many people have the wrong idea that there is something they can or must do to be saved. There is nothing we can do to make ourselves acceptable to God. However, the wrong things we do (sins) are NOT the thing that is keeping us from being accepted by God today. No, the thing that keeps us from being accepted by God is – unbelief.

The sins of all people, for all time, have already been paid for by Jesus Christ. When Jesus Christ died on the cross He bore the sins of all mankind. Jesus Christ shed His blood and died in our place, was buried, and rose to life again three days later. Our sins are paid for, but in order to be forgiven, we have to believe what Jesus Christ did.

The perfect Son of God became sin for us, so that we could receive His righteousness. "For he hath made him to be sin for us, who knew no sin; that we might be made the righteousness of God in him" (2 Cor. 5:21).

Unbelief is the only thing that separates us from eternal life with God. But God loves us and wants us to believe so He gently invites us to put our faith in what Jesus has done. We need to put our trust in who Christ is and what He has done for us. "In whom [Jesus] ye also <u>trusted</u>, after that ye heard the word of truth, the gospel of your salvation: in whom also after that ye believed, ye were sealed with that holy Spirit of promise" (Eph. 1:13).

Once we stop trusting in ourselves and place our trust in Jesus we are sealed with the Holy Spirit as a guarantee that we will spend eternity with God. "Which is the earnest [down payment] of our inheritance until the redemption of the purchased possession [the believer at the Rapture], unto the praise of his glory" (Ephesians 1:14).

A Primer with Pictures for How to Rightly Divide the Word of Truth

All the children of Adam are helpless. We inherited Adam's spiritual deadness ". . . by one man [Adam] sin entered into the world, and death by sin; and so death passed upon all men, for that all have sinned" (Rom. 5:12).

We cannot save ourselves. We are spiritually dead. But once we believe, we instantly become spiritually alive to God by <u>His power</u>. "And you hath he quickened [made alive], who were dead in trespasses and sins" (Eph. 2:1).

When we believe, we are taken out of Adam and placed into Jesus Christ. "For as in Adam all die, even so in Christ shall all be made alive" (1 Cor. 15:22). We cannot see or feel this happening, we must take it by faith in what God says in His word. We must trust in what Jesus did and His merit, not in ourselves. From the moment we believe we are "complete in him" (Col. 2:10).

Spiritually we are translated out of Adam and into His dear Son, Jesus. "Who hath delivered us from the power of darkness, and hath translated us into the kingdom of his dear Son" (Col. 1:13).

We are NOT accepted by God in ourselves, but we are accepted by the Father in His beloved Son. "To the praise of the glory of his grace, wherein he hath made us <u>accepted in the beloved</u>" (Eph. 1:6).

Christ paid for us with <u>His blood</u>. "In <u>whom we have redemption through his blood</u>, the forgiveness of sins, according to the riches of his grace" (Eph. 1:7).

We are baptized (identified) into Christ. "For as many of you as have been baptized into Christ have put on Christ" (Gal. 3:27).

Now when God sees us, He sees Jesus. God loves His Son more than anything, and we are in Him. There is no safer place to be.

God is one in three Persons: God the Father, God the Son, and God the Holy Ghost (Spirit). It was the Second Person of the Godhead who "took upon him the form of a servant, and was made in the likeness of men" (Phil. 2:7).

To be saved we need to believe the gospel (good news) of our salvation "how that [by crucifixion] Christ died for our sins according to the scriptures; And that he was buried, and that he rose again the third day according to the scriptures" (1 Cor. 15:3, 4).

Once we believe this gospel our sins are judged at the cross, and we will not be judged by them again. Thank You, Lord!

If we are in Christ, we are judged by His works; if we are in Adam, we are judged by our own works.

Our problem was that we inherited Adam's sinfulness and also commit our own sins, but by faith in Christ, we are justified freely. "Being justified freely by his grace through the redemption that is in Christ Jesus" (Rom. 3:24).

Jesus obeyed. "For as by one man's disobedience many were made sinners, so by the obedience of one shall many be made righteous" (Rom. 5:19).

Jesus died in our place. He took the payment we deserved. His <u>blood</u> paid for our sins. We receive the gift of eternal life. "For the wages of sin is death; but the <u>gift</u> of God is eternal life through Jesus Christ our Lord" (Rom. 6:23).

When we trust in what Jesus Christ has done for us, a transaction occurs: our sins are placed on Jesus Christ, and we receive His righteousness. Please, put your trust in Jesus now, for we do not know what tomorrow may bring.

God's Secret
A Primer with Pictures for How to Rightly Divide the Word of Truth
© Copyright 2017 by Marianne Manley
Pictures used by permission or public domain.
The picture "Simeon's Moment" in the FUTURE section is painted by my favorite artist, Ron DiCianni. This book is in no way endorsed or sponsored by CreateSpace, Amazon, or their affiliates.

Permission is granted to use any and all contents of this book.
All scripture references are taken from the King James Bible.
Please note that the KJB does not capitalize the pronoun names for God. Furthermore, the KJB does not use quotation marks but begins a quote with a capital letter.

A note to the reader:
This book is designed to be read from beginning to end. Please do not be discouraged if you do not understand everything right away. Get the overview of the Bible first, then later you can go back to the unclear part to understand it better. I pray that everything will become clear to you as you <u>read on</u>.

God's Secret

A Primer with Pictures for How to Rightly Divide the Word of Truth

by Marianne Manley

A Primer with Pictures for How to Rightly Divide the Word of Truth

Acknowledgement

I am grateful for the support of my dear husband Chuck (who loves me unconditionally) and my children while writing this book. I would like to thank some of the many grace pastors and teachers who have helped me understand God's word. In particular, Les Feldick, Richard Jordan, Rodney Beaulieu, Rick Jordan, Eric Neumann, Henry Meneses, Nathan Cody, David Reid, and David O'Steen. I also want to thank Maureen Parker for proofreading this book and her help in editing. I would like to thank Tiffany Hanson for her help with the format and putting the book up on CreateSpace. I would also like to thank David Jolley, and my friends who want to remain unmentioned, for the use of their wonderful pictures and memes.

To God be the glory!

This book was made possible because of God's word, excellent Bible teachers, and the help of the Holy Spirit.

"That, according as it is written, He that glorieth, let him glory in the Lord" (1 Cor. 1:31).

The King James Bible is our final authority in all matters of faith and practice.

Before God made the Heaven and the Earth, He had a "SECRET."

This secret was a "mystery . . . hid in God" (Eph. 3:9), kept secret since "before the foundation of the world" (Eph. 1:4).

Mankind is not very good at keeping secrets, but God is. "The SECRET things belong unto the LORD our God" (Deut. 29:29).

God's Secret

Table of Contents

PAST 21
- God Creates Heaven and Earth 21
- Satan Falls 21
- Adam and Eve (4,000 BC) 22
- The Fall of Mankind 23
- The Promise of the Redeemer 25
- The Flood (about 2,400 BC) 26
- The Tower of Babel (about 2,200 BC) 27
- What Happened to the Gentiles? 28
- The Call of Abraham (2,000 BC) 29
- Moses (1,500 BC) 31
- Giving Israel the Law 32
- **THE KINGDOM IS PROMISED** 34
- David King of Israel (1,000 BC) 34
- God's People Go into Captivity 35
- Daniel, in Captivity, Gives Israel the Timeline 35
- **THE KINGDOM OF HEAVEN IS AT HAND** 37
- **JESUS CHRIST BEGINS HIS EARTHLY MINISTRY** 37
- John the Baptist (30 AD) 37
- Jesus is the Promised SEED of the Woman 39
- The First Coming of the King of the Jews (33 or 34 AD*) 40
- He is Risen 45
- One Year Extension of Mercy for Israel 46
- **THE KINGDOM IS OFFERED** 47
- Jesus Christ is Ready to Ascend into Heaven 47
- The Coming of the Holy Spirit 48
- The Holy Ghost's Renewed Offer of the Earthly Kingdom 49
- The Stoning of Stephen 51

PRESENT 54
- **THE RISEN LORD JESUS CHRIST BEGINS HIS MINISTRY FROM HEAVEN** 54
- **THE PROPHESIED EARTHLY KINGDOM IS POSTPONED** 54
- The Mystery (Secret) of Christ is Revealed 54
- The Salvation of Saul of Tarsus (AD 35) 55
- The Ministry of Paul, the Apostle of the Gentiles 57
- Paul's First Apostolic Journey 58
- The Jerusalem Council 60
- Paul's Second Apostolic Journey 65

- **Paul's Third Apostolic Journey** 66
- **The Formation of the Body of Christ** 70
- **Acts is a Book of Transition** 73
- **The Mystery** 75
- **DUE TIME** 76
- **What was the SECRET?** 77
- **My Gospel** 79
- **THE SECRET** 80
- **New Creatures, Ambassadors** 83
- **What is Satan's Policy of Evil in this Dispensation?** 84
- **The Rapture** 88

FUTURE 89
- **KINGDOM ESTABLISHED** 89
- **The Tribulation** 91
- **Christ's Second Coming** 92
- **The Millennial Reign of Christ** 94
- **Satan Loosed** 95
- **The Great White Throne Judgment** 96
- **New Heaven and New Earth** 97
- **The Dispensation of the Fullness of Times** 97
- **God's Twofold Plan and Purpose** 97
- **The Kingdom of God** 98

Afterword 99

Appendix 101

Why I Use the King James Bible 102

The Faith of Jesus 110

About the Author 114

PAST

Genesis to Mid Acts (the fall of Israel occurred in Acts 7)
In the past, most Gentiles had no hope.
"Wherefore remember, that ye *being* in TIME PAST Gentiles in the flesh, who are called Uncircumcision by that which is called the Circumcision in the flesh made by hands; That at that time ye were without Christ, being aliens from the commonwealth of Israel, and strangers from the covenants of promise, <u>having no hope</u>, and <u>without God in the world</u>" (Ephesians 2:11, 12).

God Creates Heaven and Earth

"In the beginning God created the <u>heaven and the earth</u>" (Genesis 1:1). God immediately begins to focus on the Earth "And <u>the earth</u> . . ." (Gen. 1:2).

Both Heaven and Earth are organized into levels of governmental authority. There are thrones, dominions, principalities and powers in both spheres: "For by him were all things created, that are in HEAVEN, and that are in EARTH, visible and invisible, whether *they be* <u>thrones</u>, or <u>dominions</u>, or <u>principalities</u>, or <u>powers</u>: all things were created by him, and for him" (Col. 1:16).

Satan Falls

God had an adversary, Lucifer, "the anointed cherub that covereth" (Ezek. 28:14). Lucifer had an important job, he was perfect until evil was found in him, and he became Satan "Thou *wast* perfect in thy ways from the day that thou wast created, TILL INIQUITY WAS FOUND IN THEE" (Ezek. 28:15).

Lucifer is Satan (Isa. 14:12). Lucifer means "light-bearer." Satan may be light on the outside, but inside he is dark. Lucifer said, "**I will be like the most High**" (Isa. 14:14). The reason for Satan's long warfare against God is that he wants to rule and be worshipped as "possessor of heaven and earth."

Some time before he appeared in the Garden of Eden, Satan was cast out of heaven to the earth. Jesus said, "I beheld Satan as lightning fall from heaven" (Luke 10:18). Satan is "the god of this world" (2 Cor. 4:4).

We live in the "present evil world" (Gal. 1:4). The world system is organized on the principle of force, greed, selfishness, ambition, and sinful pleasure, and is a result of fallen man's captivity to Satan and his own sinful fleshly nature.

Satan had to leave God's presence and one-third of the angels followed him out of the third heaven. The second heavens became "not clean" (Job 15:15). The sky around the earth is the first heaven. Satan also became "the prince of the power of the air" (Eph. 2:2).

Adam and Eve (4,000 BC)

God made Adam and Eve and gave them dominion over the earth "And God said, Let us make man in **OUR IMAGE**, after our likeness: and let them have **DOMINION** . . . So God created man in his *own* image, in the image of God created he him; male and female created he them" (Genesis 1:26, 27). The triune God made mankind so that they could join in their loving fellowship. So that God could love them, and that they would willingly love and worship Him in return.

Adam and Eve were to reign over the Earth, bear children, set up a kingdom and take dominion "And God blessed them, and God said unto them, **Be fruitful**, and **multiply**, and **replenish the earth**, and **subdue it**: and have **dominion** over . . . **every living thing that moveth upon the earth**" (Gen. 1:28).

God gave one rule for Adam to freely and lovingly obey. God was very clear. "And the LORD God commanded the man, saying, Of every tree of the garden thou mayest FREELY eat: **But of the tree of the knowledge of good and evil, thou shalt NOT EAT of it: for in the day that thou eatest thereof thou shalt SURELY DIE**" (Gen. 2:16, 17).

God's Secret

The Fall of Mankind

Satan targets Eve. Satan continued his plan of evil against God by questioning God's word, and the woman subtracts and adds to God's word.

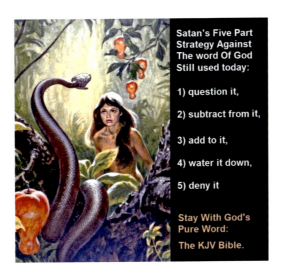

Satan (through the shining serpent) with one question to Eve, succeeded in beguiling (tricking) her. By his subtlety, Satan achieved the fall of Adam and the fall of the human race. "Now the serpent was more subtil than any beast of the field which the LORD God had made. And he said unto the woman, <u>Yea, hath God said</u> [questioned God's word], Ye shall not eat of every tree of the garden?" (Gen. 3:1).

"And the woman said unto the serpent, We may eat [she left out "freely"] of the fruit of the trees of the garden: But of the fruit of the tree which *is* in the midst of the garden, God hath said, Ye shall not eat of it, neither shall ye <u>touc</u>h it [she added "touch"], lest ye die" (Gen. 3:2, 3).

The shining serpent (acting on behalf of Satan) "that old serpent" (Rev. 12:9) lied. He tricked Eve into thinking that she and Adam could be as gods (just like Satan wanted to be "like" the most High God, possessor of heaven and earth).

Notice that God's word was changed by both the serpent and Eve. God has said several times in the Bible that no one should add or subtract from His word. "Ye shall <u>not add</u> unto the <u>word</u> which I command you, neither shall ye <u>diminish</u> *ought* from it . . ." (Deut. 4:2) (see Prov. 30:6 and Rev. 22:18, 19).

Satan lied to Eve, denying God's word. "And the serpent said unto the woman, Ye shall <u>**NOT SURELY DIE**</u> [Satan lied, that is the opposite of what God said]: For God doth know that in the day ye eat thereof, then your eyes shall be opened, and ye shall be as gods [Satan enticed her with the same desire that caused his fall], knowing good and evil" (Gen. 3:4, 5).

Eve fell for the lie in three ways (compare with 1 John 2:16): "And when the woman saw that the tree *was* good for food [lust of the flesh], and that it *was* pleasant to the eyes [lust of the eyes], and a tree to be desired to make *one* wise [pride of life], she took of the fruit thereof, and did eat, and gave also unto her husband with her; and he did eat" (Gen. 3:6).

Mankind forfeited their dominion of the earth which passed to Satan, "the god of this world" (2 Cor. 4:4). Mankind was separated from God, and all creation fell into a sinful state (Rom. 5:12, 8:22).

God had a problem: how can He remain just, and redeem mankind while allowing them free will?

God's Secret

The Promise of the Redeemer

God promised that the Redeemer would come from the "seed of the woman." Speaking to the serpent God said, "<u>And I will put enmity [constant conflict] between thee and the woman, and between thy seed and her seed; it shall bruise thy head, and thou shalt bruise his heel</u>" (Gen. 3:15).

Would God be able to use Satan's evil to find out who really loved him willingly?

Immediately, Adam and Eve realized they were naked and sewed fig leaves together to try to cover their nakedness (spiritual death). They had most likely been clothed with light before they transgressed God's command (Psalms 104:2). Their light went out! Their effort to become righteous by covering themselves is a picture of mankind trying to be righteous by their own works, religion. Clothes made from leaves do not last and are not very sturdy.

God killed some innocent animals to cover them with skins. This illustration depicts the necessity of shedding innocent blood for sin. We need to be covered with God's righteousness to be accepted by holy God.

The <u>scarlet thread of the redeeming blood is a continual theme throughout the Bible culminating in the perfectly satisfying sacrifice of God the Son upon the cross</u> (Romans 3:24-26; 1 Peter 1:18-19).

Sadly, Adam and Eve had to leave the Garden of Eden, so they would not eat of the Tree of Life and live forever in their fallen state. "So he drove out the man; and he placed at the east of the garden of Eden Cherubims, and a flaming sword which turned every way, to keep the way of the tree of life" (Genesis 3:24).

Just as God had said Adam and Eve began to die as soon as they sinned. They not only <u>died spiritually</u> when they disobeyed God's word but also started <u>dying physically</u>. Adam was 930 years old when he finally died. Adam and Eve also lost their face to face fellowship that they enjoyed with the Lord God in the garden.

Besides <u>spiritual</u> and <u>physical death</u> there is a death called the "<u>second death</u>" (this is where unbelievers go after they are judged at the Great White Throne Judgment). This second death occurs when "death and hell" are cast into the

Lake of Fire. Adam and Eve avoided that death because they believed what God said. Adam demonstrated his faith when he called his wife Eve, the "mother of all living" (Gen. 3:20). Adam believed life would come through Eve as God had said. Eve showed her faith when she thought Cain may be the Redeemer: Gen. 4:1 . . . I have gotten a man from the LORD. (Instead Cain turned out to be a type of Antichrist; he murdered his faithful brother, Abel.)

Adam and Eve became the first believers destined to be resurrected and to enter the eternal kingdom on the Earth (believers today have a different destiny, as you will discover in the PRESENT section ahead).

However, Adam and Eve passed on their spiritual death and sin nature to all mankind. The ascended LORD in heaven revealed this to Paul. "Wherefore, as by one man [Adam] sin entered into the world, and death by sin; and so death passed upon all men, for that all have sinned" (Rom. 5:12).

The Flood (about 2,400 BC)

Satan pollutes the "seed of the woman" with fallen angels to hinder the coming of the Redeemer ". . . the sons of God came in unto the daughters of men, and they bare *children* to them . . ." (Gen. 6:4).

Man is evil continually. "And GOD saw that the wickedness of man *was* great in the earth, and *that* every imagination of the thoughts of his heart *was* only evil continually" (Gen. 6:5).

Only one man, Noah, remained blameless. "But Noah found grace in the eyes of the LORD" (Gen. 6:8).

God wants to start over. "And God looked upon the earth, and, behold, it was corrupt; for all flesh had corrupted his way upon the earth . . . I will destroy them with the earth" (Genesis 6:12, 13).

God decides to send a worldwide flood, and commands Noah "Make thee an ark . . ." (Gen. 6:14).

God floods the entire earth. "And the waters prevailed exceedingly upon the earth; and all the high hills, that *were* under the whole heaven, were covered. Fifteen cubits upward did the waters prevail; and <u>the mountains were covered</u>" (Genesis 7:19, 20).

After the flood God commanded the people to spread out and fill the earth. "And God blessed Noah and his sons, and said unto them, Be fruitful, and multiply, and replenish the earth" (Gen. 9:1).

The Tower of Babel (about 2,200 BC)

Satan counters God's command at the Tower of Babel. Again people became wicked, disobeyed God, refused to spread out, made their own religion, and a tower to heaven. They did not believe nor obey God. "And the whole earth was of one language, and of one speech . . . they found a plain in the land of Shinar . . . they said one to another, Go to, let us make brick, and burn them throughly . . . Go to, let us build us a CITY and a TOWER, whose top *may reach* <u>unto heaven</u>; and let us <u>make us a name, lest we be scattered abroad upon the face of the whole earth</u>" (Gen. 11:1-4).

A Primer with Pictures for How to Rightly Divide the Word of Truth

"The Tower of Babel" by Pieter Bruegel the Elder, 1563

Because man tried to be gods, and make his own religion at the Tower of Babel, God confused their languages, making the people divide into nations. So the people spread out over the earth. "Gentiles" means nations other than Israel. "Therefore is the name of it called Babel; because the LORD did there confound the language of all the earth: and from thence did the LORD scatter them abroad upon the face of all the earth" (Gen. 11:9).

One day, God will rule from the city of the King, Jerusalem, for a thousand years.

What Happened to the Gentiles?

This is where the LORD God gave the Gentiles up, hoping to return and to save them later. Paul by revelation of Jesus Christ explains this in Romans chapter 1:18-32. "Because that, when they knew God, they glorified *him* not as God, neither were thankful; but became vain in their imaginations, and their foolish heart was darkened" (Rom. 1:21).
Romans 1:24 . . . God also gave them up to uncleanness . . .
Romans 1:26 . . . God gave them up unto vile affections . . .
Romans 1:28 . . . God gave them over to a reprobate mind . . .

The condition for the Gentiles was sad. "Wherefore remember, that ye *being* in TIME PAST Gentiles . . . having NO HOPE, and WITHOUT GOD in the world" (Eph. 2:11, 12).

God's Secret

The Call of Abraham (2,000 BC)

This time instead of destroying the wicked people of the earth with a flood, God chose to make his own <u>nation from one man, Abraham</u>.

God promised Abraham, a Gentile: "Now the LORD had said unto Abram, Get thee out of thy country [separate yourself], and from thy kindred, and from thy father's house, unto a <u>land</u> [Israel] that I will shew thee: And I will make of thee a <u>great nation</u>, and I will bless thee, and make thy name great; and thou shalt be a <u>blessing</u>: And <u>I will BLESS them that BLESS thee, and CURSE him that CURSETH thee</u>: and <u>IN THEE shall ALL FAMILIES OF THE EARTH BE BLESSED</u>" (Gen. 12:1-3).

God's Promises to Abraham:
a land
a people
a blessing
for ever (Genesis 13:15).

<u>God intended to reconcile all nations to Himself through Israel</u>. The nation Israel was to be a CHANNEL OF BLESSING to all people of the earth. "And in thy seed shall all the nations of the earth be blessed; because thou hast obeyed my voice" (Gen. 22:18). (During the prophetic program there is hope for any Gentile who shows their <u>faith</u> in Israel's God by blessing them, for example, Ruth.)

Abraham believed God and received His imputed righteousness. "And he believed in the LORD; and he counted it to him for righteousness" (Gen. 15:6). *Note: Further, and more advanced revelation about the righteousness which God imputed to Abraham's account (and other believers) is described by Paul in Romans chapter 4.

God promised "And I will make thee exceeding fruitful, and I will make NATIONS of thee, and KINGS shall come out of thee. And I will establish MY COVENANT between me and thee and thy seed after thee in their generations for an everlasting covenant, to be a God <u>unto thee, and to thy seed after thee</u>. And I will give unto thee, and to thy seed after thee, the land wherein thou art a stranger, all the LAND of Canaan, for an EVERLASTING POSSESSION; and I WILL BE THEIR GOD" (Gen. 17:6-8).

God instituted circumcision as a token for a sign of the Abrahamic covenant. "This is my covenant, which ye shall keep, between me and you and thy seed after thee; Every man child among you shall be circumcised . . . it shall be a token of the covenant betwixt me and you" (Gen. 17:10, 11).

Because God is all knowing, He predicted the length of Israel's captivity in Egypt (400 years). The author of the supernatural Bible is God, it's origin is extraterrestrial. "And he [God] said unto Abram, Know of a surety that thy seed shall be a stranger in a land *that is* not theirs [Egypt], and shall serve them; and they shall afflict them FOUR HUNDRED YEARS" (Gen. 15:13).

Abraham showed his faith in God's ability to raise up his son Isaac when he obeyed God and offered him up. God stopped him after He knew Abraham would have gone through with it. However, at the right time (Rom. 8:32), God would not spare His own Son. "And Abraham said, My son, <u>God will provide himself a lamb for a burnt offering</u> . . ." (Gen. 22:8).

Christ was to be sacrificed on Mount Moriah in a way similar to Abraham's offering of Isaac. But, as we will learn, Satan wanted to prevent that. God was not surprised because He knows the thoughts and intents of His creatures. "By faith Abraham . . . offered up his only begotten son . . . in a figure [type]" (Heb. 11:17-19; Psalms 118:27).

God changed the name of Isaac's son Jacob to Israel. Israel had twelve sons.

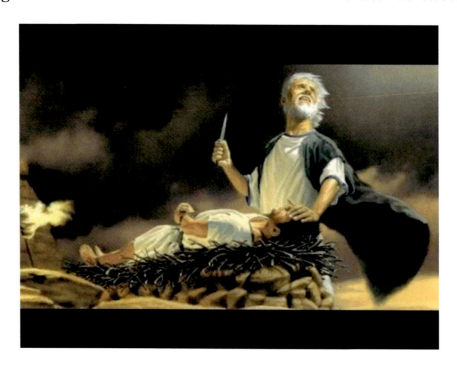

Moses (1,500 BC)

Abraham's grandson Israel and his twelve sons moved to Egypt. The twelve sons became twelve tribes. Eventually, they were made slaves in that land. After 400 years, God led His people out of Egypt using Moses, having demonstrated His power to them <u>through many signs in Egypt</u> "... the children of Israel, which went forth <u>out of the land of Egypt</u> ... <u>under the hand of Moses</u>" (Num. 33:1). God brought Israel <u>through the Red Sea</u> on their way to the <u>promised land</u>.

God commanded Moses to build a <u>tabernacle</u> after the "pattern ... shewed thee in the mount" (Ex. 25:40; Heb. 8:5). Since God knew that Israel could not keep His law, a holy place was given where the priest took the blood of the animal sacrifice to cover the sin of the people. God "passed over" their sins anticipating <u>Christ's blood</u> (Rom. 3:25).

<u>Through Moses God formed the nation of Israel in the wilderness</u>. God instituted the Law (Old Covenant) with Israel, separating them from all other nations (Lev. 20:24, 26; Deut. 4:6-8, 7:6, 26:19). Israel was to be a kingdom of priests who would be a CHANNEL OF BLESSING (Exodus 19:5, 6; Isa. 61:6; 1 Peter 2:9) to the Gentiles to save them. The law uses the <u>if-then</u> principle. "Now therefore, <u>IF ye will obey</u> my voice indeed, and <u>keep my covenant,</u> <u>THEN ye shall be a peculiar</u> [particular or unique] <u>treasure</u> unto me <u>above all people</u>: for all the earth is mine: And YE shall be unto me a KINGDOM OF PRIESTS, and an HOLY NATION ..." (Exodus 19:5, 6).

Priests were required to be ceremonially washed (baptized) with water. "And Aaron and his sons ... wash them [the priests] with water" (Ex. 29:4).

A Primer with Pictures for How to Rightly Divide the Word of Truth

Giving Israel the Law

During the exodus from Egypt God gives Israel the Ten Commandments (the Law) through Moses on Mount Sinai. However, Israel's faith fails as evidenced by them making an idol (a god they could see), a golden calf.

Israel <u>refused to believe</u> that God could help them be victorious in conquering the promised land. So the LORD made Israel wander in the wilderness for 40 years until the <u>unbelieving</u> generation died off. "And the LORD'S anger was kindled against Israel, and he made them WANDER IN THE WILDERNESS FORTY YEARS, until all the generation, that had done evil in the sight of the LORD, was consumed" (Num. 32:13).

Faith is necessary, "But without faith *it is* impossible to please *him*" (Heb. 11:6a). Israel's sacrifices and offerings had to be accompanied by faith.

God gave the children of those who wandered in the wilderness a chance to believe. Through Moses, God renewed His <u>promise</u> to set Israel above and apart from other nations. They were to be His <u>special</u> <u>people</u> from whom "the seed of the woman" would come.

<u>God reaffirmed the distinction between Israel and all other people.</u> God set Israel above all nations. "For thou *art* an holy people unto the LORD thy God the LORD thy God hath <u>CHOSEN</u> thee to be a <u>SPECIAL</u> <u>people</u> unto himself, <u>ABOVE ALL PEOPLE</u> that *are* upon the face of the earth" (Deut. 7:6).

Through Moses, God made a nation out of Israel. God led His people out of the land of Egypt and said, "Israel is my son, *even* my firstborn" (Ex. 4:22).

God, through His spokesman Moses, reviewed the law again to the next generation of Israelites. "And he wrote on the tables, according to the first writing, the TEN COMMANDMENTS, which the LORD spake unto you in the mount out of the midst of the fire in the day of the assembly: and the LORD gave them unto me [Moses]" (Deuteronomy 10:4).

Moses received the Ten Commandments

Moses promises that their days in the land will be like heaven on earth. "That your days may be multiplied, and the days of your children, in THE LAND which the LORD SWARE UNTO YOUR FATHERS TO GIVE THEM, AS THE DAYS OF HEAVEN UPON THE EARTH" (Deut. 11:21).

Christ later reveals to Paul the purpose of the Ten Commandments. No human can keep them, instead, they show mankind their need for a Redeemer ". . . for by the law *is* the knowledge of sin" (Romans 3:20).

Since no human can live up to God's standard in the Ten Commandments Israel should have said: We cannot keep the law, we need help LORD. But instead, their pride and our pride thinks we can keep the law in our flesh.

A Primer with Pictures for How to Rightly Divide the Word of Truth

THE KINGDOM IS PROMISED

David King of Israel (1,000 BC)

The seed line continues through David. God promised King David that his descendants would inherit an eternal kingdom. "And <u>THINE HOUSE AND THY KINGDOM SHALL BE ESTABLISHED FOR EVER</u> before thee: thy throne shall be established for ever" (2 Samuel 7:16).

King David

Satan Continues to Attack the Royal Seed

Satan continued to attack the "seed of the woman." At one point in Israel's history only one son remained of the "seed royal" of King David's descendants because Athaliah killed all her grandchildren except for Joash. "But when Athaliah the mother of Ahaziah saw that her son was dead, she arose and <u>destroyed all the seed royal of the house of Judah</u>. But Jehoshabeath, the daughter of the king, took <u>Joash</u> the son of Ahaziah, and stole him from among the king's sons that were slain, and put him and his nurse in a bedchamber" (2 Chronicles 22:10, 11).

God promised to deliver His children, Israel, from bondage to Satan. "But thus saith the LORD, Even <u>the captives of the mighty shall be taken away</u>, and the <u>prey of the terrible shall be delivered</u>: for I will contend with him that contendeth with thee, and <u>I WILL SAVE THY CHILDREN</u>" (Isaiah 49:25).

God's Secret

God's People Go into Captivity

The nation Israel continued to disobey God. They worshiped idols and false gods. First, the northern tribes were taken captive, and then the southern. When the tribes were released from the countries of their captivity they return to their land, rebuilt the wall around Jerusalem, and the temple.

Daniel, in Captivity, Gives Israel the Timeline

While in captivity Daniel the prophet of God (about 600 BC) wrote this prophecy: "And in the days of these kings shall the <u>GOD OF HEAVEN SET UP A KINGDOM</u>, which shall never be destroyed: and the kingdom shall <u>NOT be left to OTHER PEOPLE</u>, *but* it shall break in pieces and consume all these kingdoms, and <u>IT SHALL STAND FOR EVER</u> (Dan. 2:44).

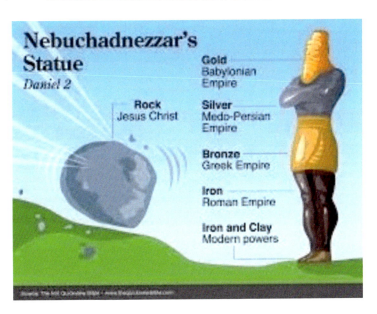

Another prophecy: "I saw in the night visions . . . *one* like <u>the Son of man came with the clouds of heaven</u>, and came to the Ancient of days, and they brought him near before him. And there was given <u>him dominion, and glory</u>, and a <u>KINGDOM</u>, that ALL people, nations, and languages, should serve him: <u>HIS DOMINION</u> *is* an <u>EVERLASTING</u> dominion, which shall not pass away, and his <u>KINGDOM</u> *that* which <u>shall not be destroyed</u> (Daniel 7:13).

In Daniel chapters 2 and 7, the <u>timeline</u> of the kingdoms of the earth is given until the coming of Messiah to set up His kingdom when the "times of the Gentiles" are over ". . . <u>until the times of the Gentiles be fulfilled</u> (Luke 21:24).

A Primer with Pictures for How to Rightly Divide the Word of Truth

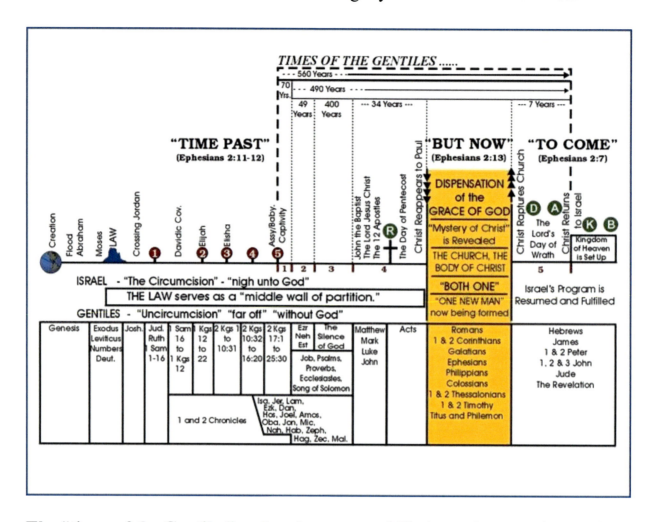

The "times of the Gentiles" end at the return of Christ at the end of the Trib. Daniel gave his people a timeline of 490 years of historical events. "Seventy weeks are determined . . ." (Dan. 9:24). The events leading up to the coming of Messiah and beyond are recorded in Daniel 9:24-27, by a series of weeks: 7x7=49 years from the building of the wall, then 434 (400 years of silence then 34 years) till Messiah came riding into Jerusalem (for a total of 483 years = 69 weeks) . . . <u>now only one more week (7 years) is left to fulfill all 490 years.</u>

<u>God's Secret</u> will explain why there is a gap between the 483 years and the last 7 years (known as Jacob's trouble mentioned in Jeremiah 30:7).

400 Years of Silence

Then there were 400 years of silence "a famine of . . . the words of the LORD" (Amos 8:11). Meanwhile, Satan had been calculating the time the Redeemer would come to Israel and had gone ahead spreading disease, evil spirits, and false religious teaching (man's rituals).

THE KINGDOM OF HEAVEN IS AT HAND

JESUS CHRIST BEGINS HIS EARTHLY MINISTRY

John the Baptist (30 AD)

The silence was broken by one crying in the wilderness and preparing the way for the King. "For this is he that was spoken of by the prophet Esaias [Greek for Isaiah], saying, The voice of <u>one crying in the wilderness, Prepare ye the way of the Lord</u>, make his paths straight" (Matt. 3:3).

God the Father sent John the Baptist. "There was a man sent from God, whose name *was* John" (John 1:6). John made the purpose of his baptism clear in John 1:31 . . . that HE should be MANIFEST to ISRAEL, therefore am I come BAPTIZING with WATER.

John the Baptist prepared Israel for the kingdom. <u>The King arrived at the perfect time prophesied by Daniel</u>. Because the time had come and their King (Jesus, the Messiah) was in their midst, John preached ". . . Repent ye: for <u>the kingdom of heaven is at hand</u> [within reach]" (Matt. 3:2). "The law and the prophets were until John: <u>since that time the kingdom of God</u> is preached, and every man presseth into it" (Luke 16:16). The prophesied time had come.

The people of Israel who believed God would keep His word and send the Redeemer for the remission (forgiveness) of their sins and set up His promised Kingdom, came to be baptized by John "confessing their sins" (Matt. 3:6).

John the Baptist pointed Jesus out to Israel.

The kingdom was not the only thing that was at hand, so too was the wrath. John warned Israel of the wrath to come. "But when he saw many of the Pharisees and Sadducees come to his baptism, he said unto them, O generation of vipers, who hath warned you to flee from the <u>WRATH TO COME</u> [the Tribulation]?" (Matthew 3:7).

The prophets spoke of things prophesied since the world began. John's father Zacharias filled with the Holy Ghost, <u>prophesied concerning the coming Redeemer</u>, saying "Blessed *be* **the Lord God of ISRAEL; for he hath <u>visited and redeemed his people,</u> And hath raised up <u>an horn of salvation</u> for us in the house <u>of his servant David</u>; As he spake by the mouth of <u>his holy prophets</u>, which have been <u>SINCE THE WORLD BEGAN</u>" (Luke 1:68-70).**

John the Baptist was the son of a priest, so he was a priest by birth. He preached in the wilderness, not temple to avoid the "generation of vipers."

John the Baptist was to baptize with water those who believed that God would keep His word to His people, making them a kingdom of priests. But he also came to identify their King. "John answered them, saying, <u>I baptize with water</u>: but there standeth one among you, whom ye know not. <u>He it is,</u> who coming after me is preferred before me, whose shoe's latchet I am not worthy to unloose" (John 1:26, 27).

The way to go from being part of the apostate nation into the believing remnant was faith demonstrated by water baptism (Num. 8:7).

John prepared the way for Jesus the Messiah of Israel and identified him to Israel, ". . . Behold the Lamb of God, which taketh away the sin of the world" (John 1:29). John bare record that Jesus was the Christ, the Son of God, saying, "<u>I saw the Spirit descending from heaven like a dove, and it abode upon him</u>. And I knew him not: but <u>he that sent me to baptize with water, the same said unto me, Upon whom thou shalt see the Spirit descending, and remaining on him, the same is he which baptizeth with the Holy Ghost. And I saw, and bare record that this is the Son of God</u>" (John 1:32-34).

John the Baptist and Jesus Christ were six months apart in age and related. The angel told Mary, the mother of Jesus, "thy cousin Elisabeth, she hath also conceived a son in her old age: and this is the <u>sixth month</u> with her, who was called barren" (Luke 1:36).

God's Secret

Jesus is the Promised SEED of the Woman

The law (not grace) was in effect when God the Son was born in Bethlehem. "But when the FULNESS OF TIME was come, GOD SENT FORTH HIS SON, MADE OF A WOMAN, made UNDER THE LAW . . ." (Gal. 4:4).

The Holy Ghost was involved in the making of the baby, <u>not</u> a human man. "And the angel answered and said unto her, <u>The Holy Ghost shall come upon thee</u>, and <u>the power of the Highest shall overshadow thee</u>: . . . that <u>holy thing which shall be born of thee shall be called the Son of God</u> (Luke 1:35).

Paul confirmed that Jesus Christ is the Seed. "Now to Abraham and his seed were the promises made. He saith not, And to seeds, as of many; but as of one, And to thy <u>SEED</u>, which <u>is CHRIST</u>" (Gal. 3:16).

Jesus Christ fulfilled many prophesies: He was born of a virgin (Isa. 7:14) in Bethlehem (Micah 5:2) of the lineage of David (Matthew 1, and Luke 3).

He came to reign. "For unto us [Israel] a child is born, unto us a son is given: and <u>the government shall be upon his shoulder</u>: and his name shall be called Wonderful, Counsellor, The mighty God, The everlasting Father, The Prince of Peace" (Isaiah 9:6).

<u>Jesus Christ lived a perfect life</u>. He finished the work given to Him by His Father. He began His ministry at the age of 30 and chose twelve disciples (Matt. 10:1-4).

A Primer with Pictures for How to Rightly Divide the Word of Truth

The First Coming of the King of the Jews (33 or 34 AD*)

*(It is interesting that the calendar does not include a year zero, 0000.)

Jesus declared Himself to be the King of the Jews, the promised Messiah. "Rejoice greatly, O daughter of Zion; shout, O daughter of Jerusalem: behold, <u>thy King cometh unto thee: he is just, and having salvation; lowly, and riding upon an ass, and upon a colt the foal of an ass</u>" (Zech. 9:9). His triumphal entry into Jerusalem was prophesied. "This is the day which the LORD hath made; we will rejoice and be glad in it" (Psalms 118:24).

He came to redeem His people (dead and alive believers), to save them from their sins. "And she shall bring forth a son, and thou shalt call his name <u>JESUS: for he shall save his people</u> [Israel] <u>from their sins</u>" (Matt. 1:21).

So that His people could also rise from the grave in the kingdom and live with Him. "<u>For I know that my redeemer liveth</u>, and that <u>he shall stand at the latter day upon the earth</u> . . . <u>in my flesh shall I see God: Whom I shall see for myself</u>, and <u>mine eyes shall behold, and not another</u> . . ." (Job 19:25-27).

This is the "resurrection of life" (John 5:29) Jesus spoke of, also known as the "first resurrection" (Rev. 20:5, 6) of the kingdom on earth believers.

God's Secret

Who did Jesus Come to Redeem?

Jesus came to save the lost sheep of Israel. He preached the gospel of the earthly kingdom. Jesus told the Syrophoenician woman "... <u>I AM NOT SENT BUT UNTO THE LOST SHEEP OF the HOUSE OF ISRAEL</u>" (Matthew 15:24). Christ's earthly ministry is recorded in Matthew, Mark, Luke, and John.

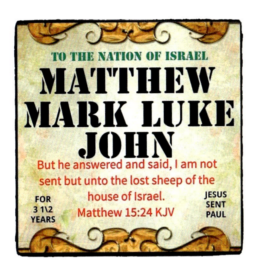

THE REASON JESUS CONFINED HIS MINISTRY TO ISRAEL WAS THAT THEY WERE TO BE THE CHANNEL OF BLESSING TO THE WHOLE WORLD.

In order for Israel to be the CHANNEL OF BLESSING, they had to be saved first. Jesus knew this and said, "... <u>salvation is of the Jews</u>" (John 4:22).

Sadly, John the Baptist was beheaded (Mark 6:24-28) by Herod, but the Jews did nothing to stop him. (Satan probably thought maybe I can get Jesus, also.)

What gospel did Jesus preach?
Jesus preached the gospel of the Kingdom. He healed everyone perfectly. "Now after that John was put in prison, Jesus came into Galilee, preaching the <u>GOSPEL OF THE KINGDOM</u> of God, and saying The time [of <u>Daniel's timeline</u>] is fulfilled, and the kingdom of God is at hand ..." (Mark 1:14, 15).

"And Jesus went about all Galilee, teaching in their synagogues, and preaching the <u>GOSPEL OF THE KINGDOM</u>, and healing all manner of sickness and all manner of disease among the people" (Matthew 4:23).

"And Jesus went about all the cities and villages, teaching in their synagogues, and preaching the GOSPEL OF THE KINGDOM, and healing every sickness and every disease among the people" (Matthew 9:35).

Jesus commissioned the twelve, gave them sign gifts, and told them to only preach to the house of Israel. "These twelve Jesus sent forth, and commanded them, saying, Go NOT into the way of the Gentiles, and into *any* city of the Samaritans enter ye NOT: But GO RATHER TO THE LOST SHEEP OF THE HOUSE OF ISRAEL. And as ye go, preach, saying, The kingdom of heaven is at hand. HEAL the sick, CLEANSE the lepers, RAISE the dead, CAST OUT devils: freely ye have received, freely give" (Matt. 10:5-8).

Jesus told His disciples that He would return before they could finish preaching the gospel all over Israel ". . . Ye shall NOT have gone over the cities of Israel, till the Son of man be COME" (Matt. 10:23).

Why has this not happened? Why did the twelve NOT finish preaching to all Israel about their Kingdom and King? Because as we shall discover Israel has been "blinded" and "cast away" for a season. Their prophesied earthly kingdom was postponed, interrupted, and put on hold (Rom. 11:7, 15, 25). But this is getting ahead of the story, so let us return to it.

Half way through His ministry, Jesus knowing that His nation had rejected Him (saying that His power is from Satan) and that He must go to the cross, begins to speak in parables so only believers will understand Him.

Sadly, Jesus was crucified by the Jews. "Then answered all the people [the Jews], and said, His blood *be* on us [the Jews], and on our [the Jews] children" (Matt. 27:25).

God's Secret

The Jews were looking for a King to rescue them physically from their Roman captors. They did not understand that **they also needed to be set free from their own sins and their captivity to Satan**. "No man can enter into a strong man's house [Satan's], and spoil his goods, except he will first bind the strong man [by the redemptive work of Christ on the cross and His resurrection]; and then he will spoil his house [take back captive Israel]" (Mark 3:27).

It was necessary to believe that Jesus is the Messiah. "I said . . . if ye believe not that I am he [Messiah the King], ye shall die in your sins" (John 8:24).

On the cross, Jesus challenged Satan. "*He* [God the Father] *is* near that justifieth me; who will contend with me? let us stand together: who *is* mine adversary? let him come near to me" (Isaiah 50:8).

Messiah's death for the sins of His people was prophesied in several places in the Bible. "And after threescore and two weeks shall Messiah be cut off, but NOT FOR HIMSELF" (Daniel 9:26). Christ died for the sins of Israel as predicted, ". . . the reproaches of them that reproached thee are fallen upon me" (Psalms 69:9). Here is another example: ". . . he *was* wounded for our transgressions [Israel's], *he was* bruised for our iniquities [Israel's]" (Isaiah 53:5). Jesus Christ knew He would be crucified (Num. 21:9; John 3:14).

In order to redeem His people, destroy Satan and death, the Lord Jesus Christ had to put on a human body. "Forasmuch then as the children are partakers of flesh and blood, he also himself likewise took part of the same; that through death he might destroy him that had the power of death, that is, the devil" (Heb. 2:14).

Out of love, the Son of God willingly laid down His life. "I lay down my life, that I may take it again . . . I have the power to lay it down, and I have the power to take it again" (John 10:17, 18). Before the cross, His disciples "understood none of these things" (Luke 18:34) pertaining to His death on the cross and resurrection even after Jesus told them ". . . they shall scourge him, and put him to death: and the third day he shall rise again" (Luke 18:33).

Satan knew that Christ was to die; that Israel was supposed to sacrifice the "lamb of God" by faith. Israel was to "bind the sacrifice with cords, even unto the horns of the altar" as Psalms 118:27 said. This is the psalm the people sang during His triumphal entry into Jerusalem (Matt. 21:9). Satan was able to convince Israel to call for His death in unbelief and demand that He would be crucified. Satan thought that this would cause God to reject His people.

A Primer with Pictures for How to Rightly Divide the Word of Truth

The King Dies for His People

While still on the cross, <u>the first cry of Jesus to the Father was NOT for Himself</u> but ". . . Father, <u>forgive them</u>; for they know not what they do . . . [meaning they are crucifying Me out of ignorance] (Luke 23:34). There is an "escape clause" for sin done in ignorance in the Jewish law (Lev. chapter 4).

<u>**At first glance, it may have appeared to Satan that the cross was his greatest triumph, but it was his demise. Jesus Christ bruised the serpent's head.**</u>

It is Finished for Many and All
In the gospels, it says that Christ came to give His life for "many" (Israel) ". . . to give his life <u>a ransom for MANY</u>" (Matt. 20:28).

But through Paul, the Apostle of the Gentiles, we learn that Christ came to be a ransom for "all." "Who gave himself <u>a ransom for ALL</u>, to be testified in due time" (1 Tim. 2:6).

Clearly "many" and "all" are NOT the same. Is there, therefore, a contradiction in the Bible? No, although there appears to be a contradiction, there is NO contradiction, because of the understanding revealed to Paul by our Lord Jesus Christ from heaven. The "secret" will clear up all apparent contradictions. Through Paul, the words Jesus spoke when He died on the cross, "<u>It is finished</u>" (John 19:30) have a broader meaning, <u>because He had completed all that was necessary to pay for all sins for all time.</u>

God's Secret

Jesus had the faith to die on the cross for everyone. Jesus believed the scriptures; and because of His faith, Jesus knew that His Father would raise Him up. He had the faith to pay the debt humanity could not pay.

He is Risen

As <u>prophesied</u> in Psalms 2, 22, 16, 69, 110; Isaiah 53, and elsewhere, the Lord Jesus Christ rose from the dead. <u>The cross, burial, and resurrection of the Lord Jesus Christ is the greatest event in history</u>!

The first day of the week women came to the tomb bringing spices to anoint the body of Jesus and saw an angel. "And the angel answered and said unto the women, . . . He is not here: for HE IS RISEN, AS HE SAID. Come, see the place where the Lord lay" (Matt. 28:5, 6). Jesus had given Israel the sign of the prophet Jonas. "For as Jonas [Jonah] was three days and three nights in the whale's belly; so shall the Son of man be three days and three nights in the heart of the earth" (Matt. 12:40). The women told His disciples this news.

Peter and the other disciple ran to the tomb. It was empty. Unfortunately, Israel still (even after His resurrection) did not believe in Jesus Christ. Sadly, "<u>He came unto his own</u> [Israel], <u>and his own received him not</u>" (John 1:11).

<u>Please notice that Matthew, Mark, Luke, and John was the continuation of the prophetic program</u>. God gave the nation of Israel one more chance to receive the Lord Jesus as their Messiah and King through the third person of the Godhead, the Holy Ghost, as the reader will discover next.

A Primer with Pictures for How to Rightly Divide the Word of Truth

One Year Extension of Mercy for Israel

Although the prophetic clock according to Daniel's timeline stopped at the cross, Israel received a bonus year of mercy from God. In addition to asking the Father to forgive them because of their ignorance while on the cross, <u>Jesus had also pleaded with the Father to give His people one more year</u> to repent and receive Him as their Messiah. ". . . A certain *man* **[God the Father] had a fig tree planted in his vineyard; and he came and sought fruit [faith] thereon, and found none. Then said he [God the Father] unto the dresser of his vineyard [God the Son], Behold, these three years I come seeking fruit on this fig tree [Israel], and find none: cut it down; why cumbereth it the ground? And he [the Son] answering said unto him, Lord, <u>let it alone this year also</u> [give Israel one more year], till I shall dig about it, and dung [fertilize by the power of the Holy Spirit]** *it*: **And if it bear fruit,** *well*: **and if not,** *then* **after that thou shalt cut it down [cut off Israel for a season]" (Luke 13:6-9).**

But Peter and the disciples of Christ, the little remnant (the little flock) did have faith in Him, so <u>the kingdom was taken from the unbelieving nation of Israel and given to the remnant of believing Israel</u>. "Therefore say I [Jesus] unto you [the religious leaders of the nation of Israel], <u>The kingdom of God shall be taken from you, and given to a nation [the little flock] bringing forth the fruits [faith] thereof</u>" (Matt. 21:43).

The little flock (believing remnant) received the kingdom. "Fear not<u>, little flock</u>; for it is your Father's good pleasure <u>to give you the kingdom</u>" (Luke 12:32).

When Peter asked Jesus what he would receive for his faithfulness Jesus answered "Verily I say unto you, That <u>ye which have followed me, in the regeneration</u> [when the Earth is regenerated in the millennium] <u>when the Son of man shall sit in the throne of his glory, ye</u> [the twelve Apostles] <u>also shall sit upon twelve thrones, judging the twelve tribes of Israel</u>" (Matthew 19:28).

Three times a year Israel was to keep a feast to the LORD. These feasts are a picture of God's plan to redeem them. Christ has already fulfilled Passover, Unleavened Bread, and Firstfruits (held in Abib, the first month). The next, Pentecost (50 days later) was fulfilled in Acts 2. The Feast of Trumpets, Day of Atonement, and Feast of Tabernacles (in the 7th month) will be fulfilled when Israel is gathered into their land, the nation is forgiven, and Messiah rules and lives with them. <u>The final feasts, as we will learn, have been postponed.</u>

THE KINGDOM IS OFFERED

Jesus had <u>warned</u> the leaders of the nation of Israel <u>not to commit the blasphemy of the Holy Ghost</u> but they were about to do it anyway "... but the blasphemy *against* the *Holy* Ghost shall not be forgiven unto men. And whosoever speaketh a word against the Son of man, it shall be forgiven him: <u>but whosoever speaketh against the Holy Ghost, it shall NOT BE FORGIVEN HIM, NEITHER IN THIS WORLD, NEITHER IN THE WORLD TO COME</u>" (Matt. 12:31, 32).

Jesus Christ is Ready to Ascend into Heaven

After His resurrection, Jesus Christ spent forty days with His disciples preparing them for their great commission. Just before His ascension into heaven while on the Mount of Olives, He spoke to them about the earthly kingdom of God. "Jesus . . . being seen of them <u>forty days</u>, and <u>speaking of the things pertaining to the kingdom of God</u>" (Acts 1:3).

Jesus told His disciples to stay in Jerusalem till they received the Holy Ghost ". . . ye shall be BAPTIZED with the HOLY GHOST not many days hence" (Acts 1:5).

The disciples had a question, they were interested in knowing if the kingdom on earth would be set up at this time. They asked Him ". . . <u>Lord, wilt thou at this time restore again the KINGDOM TO ISRAEL?</u>" (Acts 1:6)

Jesus answered that it was not for them to know. "It is not for you to know the times or the seasons, which the Father hath put in his own power [the time of the kingdom on earth is up to the Father]" (Acts 1:7).

Jesus told the little flock of believers to spread the news of the King and His Kingdom after they were empowered by the Holy Spirit (in both the south and north of Israel, and then to the rest of the earth) "... <u>ye shall receive power, after that the Holy Ghost is come upon you</u>: and ye shall be witnesses unto me both in Jerusalem, and in all Judæa, and in Samaria, and unto the uttermost part of the earth" (Acts 1:8).

Then they saw him rise up and disappear in the clouds "... when he had spoken these things, while they beheld, he was taken up; and a cloud received him out of their sight" (Acts 1:9).

Jesus ascended into heaven leaving Peter and the little flock in charge. Jesus went "into a far country" (Luke 19:12). <u>The King is in exile seated at the right hand of the Father</u>, making intercession for His people, until His enemies are made His footstool. "The LORD said unto my Lord, Sit thou at my right hand, until I make thine enemies thy footstool" (Psalms 110:1).

The Coming of the Holy Spirit

<u>Ten days later the Holy Ghost descended from heaven on the 120 gathered believers.</u> The coming of the Holy Spirit on the believers in the upper room was so loud and windy that the Jews (who were in Jerusalem from other countries to celebrate the holy day) came running to see what happened. "And when the day of Pentecost was fully come [the fulfillment of the purpose of that day], they were all with one accord in one place [the upper room]. And suddenly there came a <u>sound</u> from heaven as of <u>a rushing mighty wind</u>, and it filled all the house where they were sitting. And there appeared unto them <u>cloven tongues like as of fire</u>, and it sat upon each of them. And <u>they were all filled with the Holy Ghost, and began to speak with other tongues</u> [languages], as the Spirit gave them utterance" (Acts 2:1-4).

Curious about the wind and loud noise the men of Israel in Jerusalem for Pentecost gathered to hear what had happened as the believers came outside.

God's Secret

The Holy Ghost's Renewed Offer of the Earthly Kingdom

The men of Israel were surprised that everyone understood what was being said in their own language (Acts 2:6-8) they wondered what it meant, some mocked saying the men were drunk. Peter stood up and explained that the men were not drunk, but this is THAT which had been prophesied by Joel. "But this is that which was spoken by the prophet Joel . . . it shall come to pass in the last days, saith God, I will pour out of my Spirit . . . and your sons and your daughters shall prophesy" (Acts 2:16, 17).

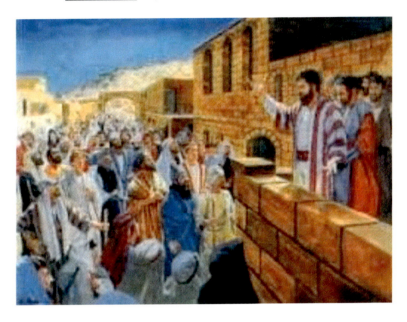

Peter preached the gospel of the kingdom on Pentecost.

Peter preached to the Jews that Jesus proved by miracles and signs that He was the Messiah and the King to sit on the throne of David. The BAD NEWS was that they had killed Him. But God had raised Jesus up again "Ye men of Israel, . . . Jesus of Nazareth . . . by miracles and wonders and signs . . . Him, ye have taken, and by wicked hands have crucified and slain: Whom God hath raised up, having loosed the pains of death: because it was not possible that he should be holden of it" (Acts 2:22-24).

Peter said that David, being a prophet, had told them that God would raise up their King ". . . raise up Christ to sit on his [David's] throne" (Acts 2:30).

The men of Israel, devastated with grief, asked what they should do. "Now when they heard *this*, they were PRICKED IN THEIR HEART, and said unto Peter and to the rest of the apostles . . . WHAT SHALL WE DO?" (Acts 2:37).

Peter answered ". . . Repent [change your mind and believe God that Jesus is the prophesied King of the Jews, the Messiah], and be baptized [in water to demonstrate your faith and be priests] every one of you in the name of Jesus Christ for the remission of sins [forgiveness], and ye shall receive the gift of the Holy Ghost [the power to witness and receive sign gifts]" (Acts 2:38). It is important to notice that Peter continued to preach repent, and be baptized just like John the Baptist. Peter called the Jews "a royal priesthood, an holy nation" (1 Peter 2:9). God's spokesman Moses had said, "ye shall be a kingdom of priest, and a holy nation" (Ex. 19:6). Three thousand believed that Jesus was the King who would set up the earthly kingdom, and were water baptized that day.

Next, Peter did his first Apostolic miracle of healing the lame man at the temple gate. The amazed Jews listened to Peter in the courtyard of the temple. Peter said that he knew that the people and their leaders killed Jesus out of ignorance, but if they would change their minds about what God said about Jesus their sins would be removed and God would send Jesus back to rule the kingdom and restore the earth, (just like all the prophets have said). "Repent ye therefore, and be converted, that your sins may be blotted out, when the times of refreshing shall come from the presence of the Lord . . . And HE SHALL SEND JESUS CHRIST, which before was preached unto you: Whom the heaven must receive until the times of restitution of all things [make things like they were when Adam was on earth], which GOD HAS SPOKEN BY THE MOUTH OF ALL HIS HOLY PROPHETS SINCE THE WORLD BEGAN" (Acts 3:19-21). God had spoken about dominion and ruling of the

The healing of the lame man at the Temple was a sign for Israel.

Earth since the days of Adam. (No one knew anything about the secret God had been keeping for more than 4,000 years.)

Another five thousand men of Israel attending the Temple (where no Gentiles were allowed) believed. But the religious leaders of Israel who represented the nation did NOT believe. Peter and the others were arrested several times and were able to preach Jesus to them but they still rejected Him as their Messiah.

As we will learn, the body of Christ is NOT to preach the coming of the earthly kingdom; but Christ crucified for ALL people. Our blessed hope is the rapture and to live with Christ forever in heaven. "For we know that if our earthly house of this tabernacle were dissolved, we have a building of God, an house not made with hands, eternal in the heavens" (2 Cor. 5:1).

The Stoning of Stephen

A year after the cross (Luke 13:6-9) Stephen, a bold Holy Spirit filled member of the believing remnant, stood up. By the power of the Holy Ghost he preached to the Jewish religious leaders. But they refused to believe that Jesus was the Messiah. They killed Stephen rejecting the Holy Ghost. This was the blasphemy of the Holy Ghost which Jesus had warned them about (Matt. 12:31, 32, see top of page 47).

The leaders of Israel refused to believe Stephen, rejecting the Holy Ghost. Stephen had told the religious leaders of Israel that they didn't believe Joseph, nor Moses until they saw them a second time (just like Israel will believe Jesus Christ the second time). "And at the second time Joseph was made known to his brethren . . . This Moses whom they refused . . . the same did God send to be a ruler and a deliverer . . ." (Acts 7:13, 35).

Stephen saw Christ in heaven standing, ready to judge Israel and pour out His wrath. "Ye stiffnecked and uncircumcised in heart and ears, ye do always resist the Holy Ghost: as your fathers did, so do ye . . . But he, being full of the Holy Ghost, looked up steadfastly into heaven, and saw the glory of God, and Jesus standing on the right hand of God, And said, Behold, I see the heavens opened, and the Son of man STANDING on the right hand of God" (Acts 7:51, 55, 56).

Why did Stephen see Jesus standing? Because God was ready to pour out His wrath. "The LORD standeth up to . . . judge the people" (Isaiah 3:13).

A Primer with Pictures for How to Rightly Divide the Word of Truth

The religious leaders of Israel were furious because of what Stephen, filled with the Holy Ghost, had told them. They pushed Stephen out of Jerusalem and <u>threw stones on him till he died</u>. <u>Saul (Paul) watched the coats</u> of the religious leaders of the nation of Israel while they ". . . cast *him* [Stephen] out of the city, and <u>stoned *him*</u>: and the witnesses <u>laid down their clothes at a young man's feet, whose name was Saul</u>" (Acts 7:58).

<u>The nation of Israel refused the renewed offer of the earthly kingdom by the Holy Ghost</u>. Now their time was up. They had <u>three strikes</u> and now they were out! <u>First</u>, they <u>rejected the Father</u> when they allowed John the Baptist to be beheaded. <u>Second</u>, they <u>rejected the Son</u> when they crucified their Messiah. <u>Third</u>, they <u>rejected the Holy Ghost</u> speaking through Stephen when they stoned him. It seemed as if God's plans for His chosen nation had all failed.

Satan probably thought he had won this time. Saul hated the church.

<u>With zeal for God, Saul persecuted the believing remnant, the little flock</u> ". . . Saul was consenting unto his [Stephen's] death. And at that time there was a great persecution against the church which was at Jerusalem; and they were all scattered abroad throughout the regions of Judæa and Samaria, <u>except the apostles</u> . . . As for <u>Saul, he made havock of the church</u>, entering into every house, and haling men and women committed *them* to prison" (Acts 8:1, 3).

Note: <u>A church is just a called out assembly</u>, a congregation. Three are mentioned in the Bible: the "church in the wilderness" (Acts 7:38) led by Moses, the church of the little flock at Jerusalem (Matt. 16:18; Acts 8:1), and the Church, the body of Christ (Eph. 1:22, 23; Col. 1:18).

God's Secret

Saul told King Agrippa, "in Jerusalem . . . <u>many of the saints did I shut up in prison</u>, having received authority from the chief priests; and <u>when they were put to death, I gave my voice against</u> *them* . . . I <u>punished them oft</u> in every synagogue, and <u>compelled</u> *them* to blaspheme; and <u>being exceedingly mad against them</u>, I persecuted them even unto strange cities" (Acts 26:10, 11).

Because the leaders of the nation of Israel did not believe that Jesus was the Messiah they could NOT be the CHANNEL OF BLESSING at this time.

Judgment was pending, but instead of pouring out His prophesied wrath, <u>God surprised everyone</u> (even Satan and his fallen angels). <u>God had kept a SECRET that no one knew up until this point in history.</u> God had kept this SECRET in Himself since "<u>. . . before the foundation of the world</u>" (Eph. 1:4).

God did something <u>totally un-prophesied</u>, He saved his worst enemy (who had watched the coats of those who stoned Stephen) and persecuted the little flock, Saul of Tarsus.

Now Jesus interrupts "Prophecy" and inserts the "Mystery" (the yellow part on the timeline pictured below).

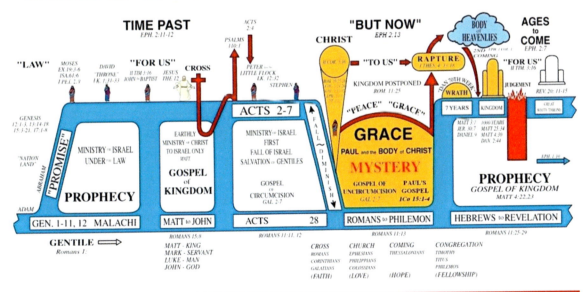

A Primer with Pictures for How to Rightly Divide the Word of Truth

PRESENT

Romans to Philemon, (Acts 9-28 is the transition from Peter to Paul). Gentiles NOW have hope because of the <u>blood of Christ</u>.
"<u>BUT NOW</u> [these two words indicate a dispensational change] in Christ Jesus ye who sometimes were far off are made nigh by the <u>blood</u> of Christ" (Ephesians 2:13).

THE RISEN LORD JESUS CHRIST BEGINS HIS MINISTRY FROM HEAVEN

THE PROPHESIED EARTHLY KINGDOM IS POSTPONED

Satan was about to be the most surprised creature in heaven and on earth. God had a secret plan and decided to use His enemy Saul to help execute it. As mentioned, God did not send His prophesied WRATH on the people of the earth. Instead He saved the chief of sinners, showed him grace, and appointed him to be His minister. "That I should be the <u>minister of Jesus Christ to the Gentiles</u>, ministering the gospel of God, that the offering up of the Gentiles might be acceptable, being sanctified by the Holy Ghost" (Rom. 15:16).

<u>The Lord Jesus Christ interrupted prophecy, inserted the dispensation of the grace of God in which we now live, and formed the body of Christ</u>. Jesus Christ chose Paul as His spokesperson for His ministry from heaven (just like Moses had been the main spokesperson for Him during Israel's formation as a nation and the giving of the law). "If ye have heard of the DISPENSATION OF THE GRACE OF GOD which is <u>given me</u> [Paul] <u>to you-ward</u>" (Eph. 3:2).

The Mystery (Secret) of Christ is Revealed

<u>The rapture is exclusively found in Paul's epistles</u>. <u>The dispensation of grace and the formation of the Church</u>, the body of Christ both began with Paul's salvation on the road to Damascus. <u>It will end at the rapture</u>. "For the Lord himself shall descend from heaven with a shout . . . then we . . . shall be caught up . . . to meet the Lord in the air" (1 Thess. 4:16, 17). Christ has given us a blessed hope and we look for His appearing.

God's Secret

The Salvation of Saul of Tarsus (AD 35)

Suddenly (without being prophesied in the word of God) Jesus Christ returned from heaven and appeared in the air to Paul and spoke with him. Saul (Paul) explained to king Agrippa what happened: ". . . I persecuted *them* [those who believed that Christ was their King] even unto strange cities . . . I went to Damascus with authority and commission from the chief priests . . . At midday, I saw . . . a light from heaven, above the brightness of the sun, shining round about me and them which journeyed with me. And when we were all fallen to the earth, I heard a voice speaking unto me, and saying in the Hebrew tongue, Saul, Saul, why persecutest thou me? *it is* hard for thee to kick against the pricks [your conscience]. And I said, Who art thou, Lord? And he said, I am Jesus whom thou persecutest. But rise, and stand upon thy feet: for I HAVE APPEARED TO THEE FOR THIS PURPOSE, TO MAKE THEE A MINISTER and a WITNESS BOTH OF THESE THINGS WHICH THOU HAST SEEN, and of those THINGS in the which I WILL APPEAR TO THEE; Delivering thee from the people [Israel], and *from* the Gentiles, unto whom NOW I send thee, To open their eyes, *and* to turn *them* FROM DARKNESS TO LIGHT, and *from* the POWER of SATAN UNTO GOD, that THEY MAY RECEIVE FORGIVENESS OF SINS, and inheritance among them which are sanctified by FAITH WHICH IS IN ME" (Acts 26:11-18).

*Notice that Jesus just said that the "faith" was in Him (more on that later).

Stephen had seen Jesus standing ready to execute His WRATH that John the Baptist had warned the unbelieving nation of Israel of (Matt. 3:7; Isaiah 3:13). But instead, the ascended, risen Lord Jesus dramatically appeared to Saul . . . and commissioned him to save all men. "But the Lord said . . . he [Paul] is a chosen vessel unto me, to bear my name before the GENTILES, and KINGS, and the CHILDREN OF ISRAEL" (Acts 9:15).

Instead of the <u>prophesied WRATH</u>, God at present offers grace and peace to all who will believe. "To all . . . GRACE AND PEACE from God our Father, and the Lord Jesus Christ" (Rom. 1:7).

<u>**Jesus started something brand new with Paul.**</u> **Jesus Christ made Paul, the Apostle of the Gentiles. "<u>For I speak to you Gentiles, inasmuch as I am the APOSTLE of the GENTILES, I magnify mine office</u>" (Rom. 11:13). An apostle is someone who is first sent with a message. Christ sent Peter, and then He sent Paul.**

<u>**Christ gave the mystery revelation to Paul progressively**</u>**, appearing and speaking to him several times ". . . acknowledge that <u>the things that I write unto you are the commandments of the Lord</u>" (1 Cor. 14:37). Then again ". . . <u>I will COME TO VISIONS and revelations of the Lord</u>" (2 Cor. 12:1).**

<u>**Jesus spoke to Paul at other times,**</u> **in Acts 22 Jesus said he should "depart" from Jerusalem for He would send him to the Gentiles. Christ told Paul that His grace was "sufficient" for him in 2 Cor. 12.**

The Ministry of Paul, the Apostle of the Gentiles

Paul's distinctive ministry was full of difficulties and sufferings: "he must suffer for my name's sake" (Acts 9:16). After being saved, Paul spent three years in Damascus and Arabia learning from Jesus. **Jesus kept His Apostle, Paul, separate from the twelve because He gave Paul a different message.** "But when it pleased God, who separated me . . . To reveal his Son in me, that I might preach him among the heathen; immediately **I conferred not with flesh and blood:** Neither went I up to Jerusalem to them which were apostles before me; but **I went into Arabia, and returned again unto Damascus. Then after three years I went up to Jerusalem to see Peter**, and abode with him fifteen days" (Gal. 1:15-18).

Paul had to escape from Damascus in a basket because the Jews wanted to have him caught. "In Damascus the governor . . . with a garrison, desirous to apprehend me: And through a window in a BASKET was I let down by the wall, and escaped his hands" (2 Cor. 11:32, 33).

Paul went to Jerusalem to join the "little flock" of believers there. But **they were afraid of him since he had persecuted them in the past.** Barnabas, a little flock believer, became Paul's friend and introduced him to the others. Paul began to preach Jesus in Jerusalem. But **he soon ran into trouble** with the unbelieving Jews which spoke Greek since they "**went about to slay him**" (Acts 9:29). For his safety, **the believers sent Paul to his hometown, Tarsus.**

A Primer with Pictures for How to Rightly Divide the Word of Truth

News reached Peter and the little flock that many in Antioch of Syria believed in Jesus so they sent Barnabas to investigate. When Barnabas saw that many Jews and Gentiles believed at Antioch, he went to find Paul because he remembered that Jesus had made him the Apostle of the Gentiles.

The church at Antioch flourished. After a year the Holy Ghost let them know that He wanted Paul and Barnabas to go and preach in other places.

Paul's First Apostolic Journey

Paul and Barnabas took their first Apostolic journey with John Mark to Cyprus (the home of Barnabas) and Asia Minor (Pamphylia, Galatia, in modern day Turkey). John Mark, the nephew to Barnabas, decided to leave when the going got tough early in their travels. Their method of preaching was first to the Jews in their Synagogues and then to the Gentiles. However, they ran into strong opposition from both the Jews and the Gentiles.

Many Jews were angry because <u>they thought Paul was speaking against Moses</u> and the law. <u>They despised Paul because he preached justification by faith alone in what Christ had done,</u> <u>apart from Israel being God's CHANNEL OF BLESSING and the keeping of the law of Moses</u>. They wanted to stone Paul to death because he said, "by him all that believe <u>are justified from all things, from which ye could not be justified by the law of Moses</u>" (Acts 13:39).

God's Secret

On the other hand, <u>the Gentiles were very entrenched in their false gods and idol worship</u>. After Paul healed a man born crippled, they even tried to worship Paul and Barnabas. Paul stopped them saying we are only men, worship God. However, the unbelieving Jews arrived from the other towns that Paul and Barnabas had preached in. They persuaded the Gentiles to stone Paul.

Stoned, drug out of town and left for dead in Lystra, Paul's friends were surprised when he revived. The brave apostles returned through the same towns where they had told the people about Jesus. They encouraged all the believers in their faith. Then they assisted the church groups in appointing older faithful men to help them continue to trust in what Jesus had done.

Paul and Barnabas returned to their headquarters in Antioch (in Syria), and told their friends how God had helped them start the churches on their trip.

Paul preached that nothing people do saves them, only faith in what Jesus has done matters. <u>We are justified by His faith</u>. It is our faith "in" the faith "of" Jesus that matters. (All modern bibles except the King James Bible change the little word "of" to "in"). "Knowing that a man is not justified by the works of the law, but by the <u>faith OF Jesus Christ</u>, even we have <u>believed IN Jesus Christ</u>, that we might be justified by the <u>faith OF Christ</u>, and not by the works of the law: for by the works of the law shall no flesh be justified" (Gal. 2:16).

The doctrine of the faith "of" Jesus is changed in all modern Bibles. They replace the word "of" with "in" removing the fact that it was Jesus who had the faith, putting the emphasis on the believer, NOT Christ. We only put our faith "in" what He has already DONE. Jesus had to trust and obey all that the Father told Him. He had to live a perfect life, teach the believing in Israel, and demonstrate who He was. Then He had to believe that His death would satisfy the righteous requirement of God the Father. He also had to go through with dying, believing that His Father would raise Him up from the dead. The little word "of" makes a big difference. See Faith of Jesus in the Appendix, pg. 110.

Paul was furious when some believers from the little flock in Jerusalem came to Antioch and told the believers there that they had to be circumcised to be saved ". . . Except ye be circumcised after the manner of Moses, ye cannot be saved" (Acts 15:1). Paul said that if people are circumcised they are showing their lack of faith in Christ. "Behold, I Paul say unto you, that if ye be circumcised, CHRIST shall PROFIT YOU NOTHING" (Gal. 5:2).

Paul preached that Christ did it all and that circumcision was not important. Paul wrote, "And I, brethren, if I yet preach circumcision, why do I yet suffer persecution? then is the offence of the cross ceased" (Gal. 5:11). But the Jews had been taught circumcision was the sign of the covenant between them and God in Genesis 17.

A big argument broke out. Finally, Jesus instructed Paul to go up to Jerusalem to settle the matter "I went up by revelation, and communicated unto them that gospel which I preach among the Gentiles . . ." (Gal. 2:2).

The Jerusalem Council

So (seventeen years after his conversion) Paul, Barnabas, and Titus arrived in Jerusalem and had several meetings with the little flock of believers there. Many in Jerusalem had begun to wonder why the kingdom on earth had not come saying "Where is the promise of his coming?" (2 Peter 3:4).

In the Jerusalem council, Peter spoke up on Paul's behalf. "And when there had been much disputing, Peter rose up, and said unto them . . . a good while ago God made choice . . . that the Gentiles by my mouth should hear the word of the gospel, and believe" (Acts 15:7). Peter said that God had saved Cornelius (a centurion who blessed Israel) and his household, so why should they force the Gentiles to keep the law which even the Jews could not keep?

(As we shall find out, Paul's ministry and the SECRET was about much more than Gentile salvation).

Then the council listened to Barnabas and Paul who declared what miracles and wonders God had done among the Gentiles through them "Then all the multitude kept silence, and gave audience to Barnabas and Paul, declaring what <u>miracles</u> and <u>wonders</u> God had wrought among the Gentiles by them" (Acts 15:12). The signs that Paul was doing showed that God was now working through Paul and his ministry "<u>the Jews require a sign</u> . . ." (1 Cor. 1:22). <u>Peter and Paul preached different messages to different audiences</u>.

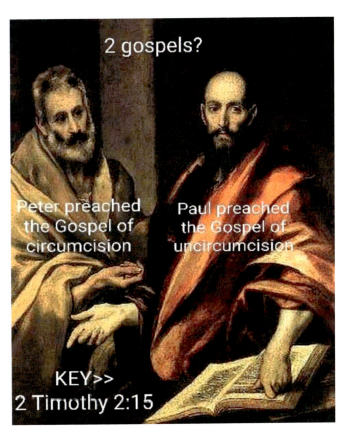

Paul explained to the little flock that <u>Good News</u>, the gospel of the grace of God, that Christ had given him. Eventually, Peter, James, John and the others of the little flock finally "saw" that the Lord Jesus Christ had given Paul a <u>different gospel and apostleship than Peter</u>. "But contrariwise, when they <u>SAW</u> that the <u>GOSPEL OF THE UNCIRCUMCISION</u> was committed unto me, as *the <u>GOSPEL</u> OF THE CIRCUMCISION* was unto Peter; (For he that wrought effectually in Peter to the <u>apostleship</u> of the circumcision [Jews], the same was mighty in me toward the Gentiles)" (Gal. 2:7, 8).

A Primer with Pictures for How to Rightly Divide the Word of Truth

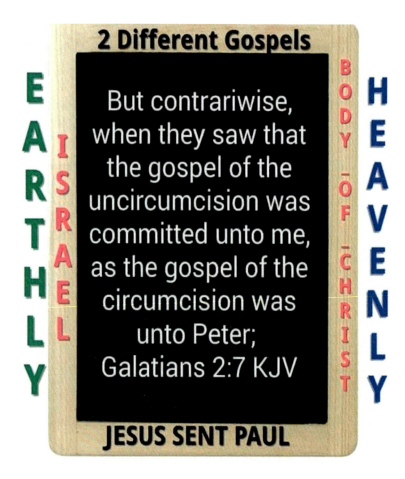

These are two different gospels, one heavenly and one earthly.

Finally, the little flock of believers "perceived" or understood the different message of grace that the ascended, risen Lord Jesus Christ in heaven had given to Paul. They may have realized that God was now doing <u>something new</u> through Paul. "And when James, Cephas [Peter], and John, who seemed to be pillars, <u>PERCEIVED THE GRACE THAT WAS GIVEN TO ME</u>, THEY GAVE TO ME AND BARNABAS the <u>RIGHT HANDS OF FELLOWSHIP</u> [made an agreement of approval in good faith]; <u>that we *should go* unto the heathen</u> [all nations], and <u>they unto the circumcision</u> [Israel]" (Gal. 2:9).

So the two groups of believers made an agreement. The little flock, who preached the gospel of the coming earthly kingdom, would go to the CIRCUMCISION, while Paul would go to the HEATHEN (all unbelievers). Those Jews and Gentiles who believed the gospel Paul preached became heaven bound members of the body of Christ.

The twelve Apostles preached to Israel, while one Apostle preached to all nations. Paul was a Jew and a Roman citizen so he was the perfect choice to preach to the body of Christ made up of both individual Jews and Gentiles.

At the Jerusalem council, James gave the final verdict. He said he was sorry that some men from their group had troubled the believers in Antioch, but that they had not sent them. "Forasmuch as we have heard, that certain which went out from us have troubled you with words, subverting your souls, saying, *Ye must* BE CIRCUMCISED, and keep the law: to whom we gave NO *SUCH* COMMANDMENT" (Acts 15:24).

James said that circumcision of the flesh was not necessary for the Gentiles' salvation. He also said that it would be good if the Gentiles would not stumble the Jews with what they ate and would avoid fornication. After shaking hands, the little flock sent a letter to the believers in Antioch. Two of their best men, Judas and Silas, accompanied Paul and his friends back to Antioch.

Many of the little flock had been wondering why the Lord was delaying sending His wrath (mentioned by John the Baptist in Matthew 3 and by Jesus Christ in Matthew 24) and His Second Coming. The answer was that the risen ascended Lord Jesus Christ had begun a new un-prophesied ministry from heaven through Paul.

A Primer with Pictures for How to Rightly Divide the Word of Truth

The twelve never fulfilled the great commission. Peter and the eleven preached the Gospel of the Kingdom. Peter's ministry was placed on hold, but it will resume in the future earthly kingdom when he is resurrected to reign with Jesus, his Messiah and King. Peter wrote to the scattered little flock of Israel believers that Jesus is longsuffering (for nearly 2,000 years so far) because He wants to save as many as possible and that they should learn from the wisdom contained in the scriptures Paul wrote.

Peter said that some of what Paul said was difficult to understand (of course Peter had been taught a different message by Jesus in His earthly ministry to Israel). "And account *that* the LONGSUFFERING of our Lord *is* SALVATION; even as our beloved brother PAUL also according to the WISDOM GIVEN UNTO HIM hath written unto you; As also in all *his* epistles, speaking in them of these things; in which are some things HARD to be understood, which they that are unlearned and unstable wrest, as *they do* also the other SCRIPTURES, unto their own destruction" (2 Peter 3:15, 16).

Jesus WAS, BUT NOW is . . .

Jesus WAS a minister to the circumcision (the nation of Israel). "Now I say that Jesus Christ WAS a minister of the circumcision [the nation of Israel] for the truth of God, to confirm the promises *made* unto the fathers [Abraham, Isaac, Jacob and his twelve sons]" (Rom. 15:8).

BUT NOW Jesus is . . .
the risen, ascended Head of the Church, the body of Christ.

What Christ ministered from heaven through Paul is our latest information. Unlike Peter, Paul said he did not follow Christ's earthly ministry, but His ministry from heaven. Paul did NOT preach what Christ taught in Matthew, Mark, Luke, and John. Paul said that we no longer follow the earthly ministry of Jesus Christ. "Wherefore henceforth know we no man after the flesh: yea, though we have known CHRIST AFTER THE FLESH, YET NOW HENCEFORTH KNOW WE HIM NO MORE" (2 Cor. 5:16).

The temporary spiritual gifts given to Paul and the body of Christ were to show Israel that God was now operating through Paul and his ministry. Signs validate a ministry. "For the Jews require a SIGN, and the Greeks seek after wisdom" (1 Cor. 1:22).

God's Secret

Paul's Second Apostolic Journey

Sometime after they returned to Antioch, Paul wanted to take another Apostolic journey to check on the churches. Barnabas insisted on bringing Mark, but Paul refused to bring him since he had deserted them on the first trip so they split up.

Paul took Silas and they were joined by Timothy in Lystra and doctor Luke in Troas. They were converting Jews and Gentiles by the power of the gospel of Christ whenever they could. They ran into trouble in Philippi where Paul and Silas were jailed. Paul said, "Believe on the Lord Jesus Christ" (Acts 16:31).

After their release more trouble followed in Thessalonica and Berea. Paul had to jump on a ship to Athens. He preached at Mars' Hill. Then Paul went to Corinth. Silas and Timothy joined him there.

Paul preached Christ crucified for our sins and risen again, wherever he went.

A Primer with Pictures for How to Rightly Divide the Word of Truth

Paul's Third Apostolic Journey

On his third Apostolic journey, Paul spent nearly three years in Ephesus. For two of those years, he taught at a school so all of Asia Minor (modern day Turkey) heard him ". . . the school of one Tyrannus. And this continued by the space of two years; so that <u>all they which dwelt in Asia heard the word of the Lord Jesus, both Jews and Greeks</u>" (Acts 19:9, 10).

This profitable ministry lasted until the silver and coppersmiths caused such an <u>uproar</u> that it was safest for him to leave. The metal workers who made shrines to the false goddess Diana were upset that Paul was making them lose customers since so many in that great city of Ephesus now trusted in the gospel of Christ. "Moreover, brethren, I [Paul] declare unto you <u>the gospel</u> which I preached unto you, which also ye have received, and wherein ye stand; <u>By which also ye ARE SAVED</u>, if ye keep in memory what I preached unto you [and do not start believing in something else such as what you have done], unless ye have believed in vain. For I [Paul] delivered unto you first of all that which I also received, how that <u>CHRIST</u> [God in the flesh] <u>DIED FOR OUR SINS</u> according to the scriptures; And that <u>he was BURIED</u>, and that <u>he ROSE AGAIN the third day according to the scriptures</u>" (1 Cor. 15:1-4).

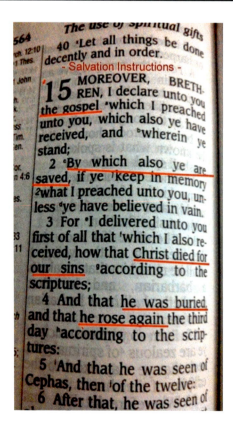

God's Secret

Paul traveled through Macedonia, Illyricum (Dalmatia, former Yugoslavia), back to Corinth in Greece. "Through mighty signs and wonders, by the power of the Spirit of God; so that from Jerusalem, and round about unto Illyricum, I have fully preached the gospel of Christ" (Rom. 15:19).

Paul heard that the unbelieving Jews in Greece planned to catch him as he was about to sail from Greece to Jerusalem, so he and his friends traveled back mostly by land. Eventually, they arrived at their destination.

In Jerusalem, Paul was arrested. This saved his life from the Jews who were beating him up. They wanted to kill him because he preached that Gentiles could be saved apart from going to God through Israel, and apart from the law. The Jews believed that they were to be the CHANNEL OF THE BLESSINGS OF ABRAHAM TO THE GENTILES. (And they will be when God resumes His dealings with Israel after the rapture.)

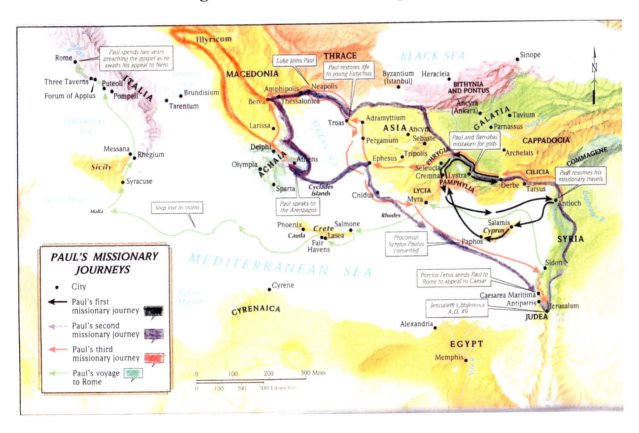

Paul was more than a "missionary" because he was the one Apostle chosen by Jesus Christ from heaven to form the body of Christ in this dispensation of grace. His journeys were "Apostolic," he alone says "according to my gospel."

After more than two years of being a prisoner in Israel under procurator Felix, and then Festus, Paul was sent to Rome as a prisoner. On the way, they suffered his fourth shipwreck, but everyone onboard survived.

Three days after Paul arrived in Rome under house arrest, he summoned the local Jews to come and hear his message. Most of them rejected his message. So Paul said, for the third and final time (Acts 13:46, 18:6, 28:28) from now on I am going to the Gentiles. Paul had tried to provoke the Jews to believe that God was working through him by the sign gifts he had been given, and his preaching so that they could be rescued from eternal punishment and become body of Christ members. With Paul's decision to go to the Gentiles sign gifts ended.

Paul explained that the Jews stumbled at the cross when they killed Jesus, their Messiah. **They then fell at the stoning of Stephen** (the rejection of their last offer of the kingdom through the third Person of the Godhead, the Holy Ghost). "I say then, Have they STUMBLED [at the cross] that they should fall [the stoning of Stephen]? God forbid: but *rather* through THEIR FALL SALVATION *IS COME* UNTO the GENTILES, for to PROVOKE THEM to JEALOUSY. Now if the FALL of them *be* the RICHES OF THE WORLD, and the DIMINISHING [during the Acts period] of them the riches of the Gentiles; how much more their fulness? [God is NOT finished with Israel; He is yet to bless them]" (Rom. 11:11, 12).

God's Secret

In a letter, Paul recounts some of his sufferings "Of the Jews five times received I forty *stripes* save one. Thrice was I beaten with rods, once was I stoned, <u>thrice I suffered shipwreck</u>, a night and a day I have been in the deep; *In* journeyings often, *in* perils of waters, *in* perils of robbers, *in* perils by *mine own* countrymen, *in* perils by the heathen, *in* perils in the city, *in* perils in the wilderness, *in* perils in the sea, *in* perils among false brethren; In weariness and painfulness, in watchings often, in hunger and thirst, in fastings often, in cold and nakedness. Beside those things that are without, that which cometh upon me daily, the care of all the churches [Paul prayed for the churches, and made sure they had leaders]" (2 Cor. 11:24-28).

Like Paul, our "pattern," we will suffer. But then Paul wrote, "For I reckon that the sufferings of this present time *are* not worthy *to be compared* with the glory which shall be revealed in us" (Rom. 8:18).

Paul wrote several letters; many were to the churches he had begun. The thirteen letters he wrote comprise the "sound doctrine" for the Church, the body of Christ. Paul remained on house arrest for two years. After the hearing of his defense, Paul was released.

Paul traveled to check on the churches he had begun. He may have taken his planned trip to Spain. He left Timothy in charge at Ephesus, then went to Nicopolis near Philippi, for the winter. Paul asked Titus to join him after his replacement arrived in Crete where Titus was ministering.

At some point, Paul was rearrested, brought to Rome and placed in a dungeon. He wrote his last letter to Timothy before he was executed. History says he was martyred being beheaded by Nero probably in 67 or 68 AD. Paul wrote to Timothy, "I have fought a good fight, I have finished *my* course, I have kept the faith" (2 Tim. 4:7). He had written down the foundational doctrine for the new creature, the body of Christ, just like Jesus wanted.

The Formation of the Body of Christ

The Lord Jesus Christ called Paul to build a New Agency – the Church, the body of Christ. Paul laid the foundation. Paul is the <u>masterbuilder</u> and his foundation is Jesus Christ according to the revelation of the mystery.

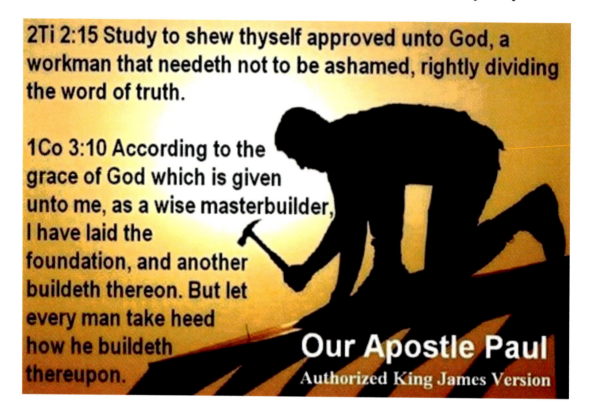

The members of the body of Christ build on the sound doctrine laid down by Paul. "According to the grace of God which is given unto me, as a wise <u>masterbuilder</u>, I have laid the foundation, and another buildeth thereon. But let every man take heed how he buildeth thereupon" (1 Cor. 3:10).

Jesus Christ began something new. "Therefore if any man be in Christ, he is a new creature: old things are passed away; behold, <u>all things are become new</u>" (2 Cor. 5:17). He formed the body of Christ, the "<u>one new man</u>" (Eph. 2:15).

- **New Apostle**
- **New Gospel**
- **New Dispensation**
- **New Agency (the body of Christ)**
- **New Audience (all people)**
- **New Destiny (Heaven)**

Before Paul no one knew that the house of God was a duplex. The blueprint for the whole other side of the building was NOT known until Christ from heaven revealed it to Paul. "And there are differences of administrations, but the same Lord" (1 Cor. 12:5). The duplex represents the family of true believers in heaven and earth.

Peter spoke to "the house of Israel" (Acts 2:36) and Paul said, "*ye* are God's building" (1 Cor. 3:9). **Jesus Christ is the foundation according to the revelation of the mystery, AND the foundation according to prophecy.** "For other <u>foundation</u> can no man lay than that is laid, which is <u>JESUS CHRIST</u>" (1 Cor. 3:11). According to prophecy, Jesus is the Rock to build that church on. "Behold, I lay in Sion a chief corner stone, elect, precious: and he that believeth on him shall not be confounded" (1 Peter 2:6). Jesus said, "upon this rock will I build my church" (Matt. 16:18). Both groups of people are redeemed by the <u>blood</u> of the Lord Jesus Christ, the Son of God.

A Primer with Pictures for How to Rightly Divide the Word of Truth

Paul was the <u>first person</u> into the body of Christ and he is our <u>pattern</u> for today ". . . I [Paul] obtained mercy, that <u>in me first</u> Jesus Christ might shew forth all longsuffering, for a <u>pattern</u> to them which should hereafter believe on him to life everlasting (1 Tim. 1:16). <u>This current Church began with him</u>.

We follow Paul to follow Christ. "Be ye followers of me, even as I also *am* of Christ" (1 Cor. 11:1). Christ made Paul the spokesman for this dispensation ". . . a dispensation *of the gospel* is committed unto <u>me</u> [Paul]" (1 Cor. 9:17).

<u>To dispense means to distribute, give out</u>. A gas station dispenses gasoline. <u>God dispenses a set of instructions for a group of people to follow for a specific period of time</u>. God never changes. But His instructions to mankind has changed over time. Some could not eat a certain fruit, one had to build an ark, another to believe that he would have descendants who would become a nation and inherit a land, etc. The two main divisions in the Bible are "prophecy" and "mystery." <u>The word "dispensation" occurs four times in the Bible</u>: Ephesians 1:10, 3:2; Colossians 1:25; 1 Corinthians 9:17. We are living in the dispensation of the grace of God.

<u>In this dispensation God is dispensing grace. His INSTRUCTION to mankind by way of His messenger Paul, is sound doctrine and to believe the gospel.</u> Anyone can be saved by believing the Good News found in 1 Cor. 15:1-4:

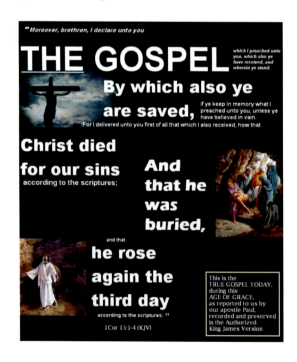

God died for our sins and rose. Believe and be saved. Faith plus nothing!

God's Secret

Today, in the dispensation of grace, God is not holding our sins against us. A person sends themselves to eternal hell not because of the wrong things he does, but because of his <u>unbelief</u> in what Christ has done for him on the cross, and His resurrection. "To wit, that God was in Christ, reconciling the world unto himself, <u>NOT IMPUTING their TRESPASSES unto them</u>" (2 Cor. 5:19).

God began a new dispensation when He saved Paul. Now, law is not in effect, but grace ". . . ye are not under the law, but under grace" (Rom. 6:14).

Paul explained that Israel is NOT the preferred nation today, but should be treated as any other nation (and be saved by the same gospel). The <u>middle wall</u> of partition between the circumcised (Israel) and the uncircumcision (the Gentiles) is broken down "For he is our peace, <u>who hath made both one</u>, and hath <u>BROKEN DOWN</u> the <u>MIDDLE WALL OF PARTITION</u> between us" (Eph. 2:14). Israel is considered to be just like any other nation today.

Jesus Christ has created a new organism of both Jews and Gentiles. Today there is no difference between individual Jews (<u>not</u> the nation) and Gentiles. "Having abolished in his flesh the enmity, *even* the law of commandments *contained* in ordinances; for <u>TO MAKE IN HIMSELF OF TWAIN</u> [individual Jews and Gentiles] <u>ONE NEW MAN</u> [the body of Christ with Jesus as the Head], *so* making peace" (Eph. 2:15).

Today we are all one body of believers in Christ. "There is NEITHER JEW NOR GREEK, there is neither bond nor free, there is neither male nor female: for ye are <u>ALL ONE in Christ Jesus</u>" (Gal. 3:28).

<u>In the beginning of his ministry, Paul went to the Jew first,</u> until the diminishing of Israel was complete in Acts 28. "For I am not ashamed of the gospel of Christ: for it is the power of God unto salvation to every one that believeth; to the JEW FIRST, and also to the Greek" (Rom. 1:16).

Acts is a Book of Transition

The book of Acts demonstrates why God is justified in setting aside the nation of Israel. First, they rejected Peter's message, and then they rejected Paul's message. Although the nation of Israel did not believe, Peter and the remnant did. The transition goes from God's man Peter to Paul. For a while, Paul had sign gifts to show the Jews that God was now working through him. "For the JEWS REQUIRE a SIGN, and the Greeks seek after wisdom" (1 Cor. 1:22).

A Primer with Pictures for How to Rightly Divide the Word of Truth

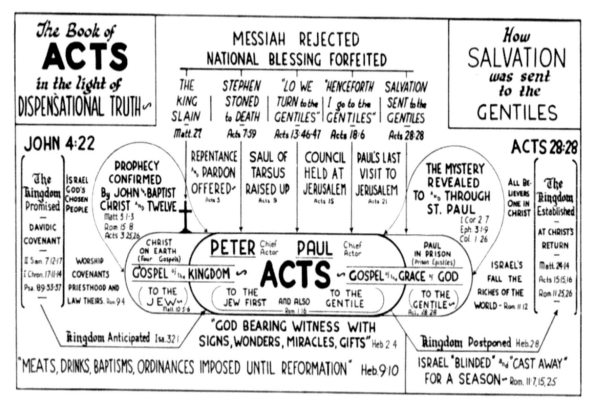

Acts, Dispensationally Considered (Vol. 1), by C. R. Stam, pg. 12

During Acts, a transition is made from Peter (and the believing remnant of Israel, the "little flock" mentioned in Luke 12:32) to Paul (and the body of Christ). The sign gifts were temporarily given to Paul and the body of Christ to show Israel that God was now operating through Paul and his ministry. The Corinthian church shared a wall with a Jewish synagogue (Acts 18:7). After three strikes the Jews were out (Acts 13:46, 18:6, 28:28). The provoking ministry (Rom. 11:11) to the Jews and sign gifts ended in Acts 28 with the complete revelation of the mystery to Paul. "But when that which is PERFECT IS COME [the complete revelation to Paul], then that which is IN PART [temporary sign gifts] shall be done away" (1 Cor. 13:10). The sign gifts also supported the Church in its infancy (1 Cor. 13:11, 12).

<u>**God postponed Peter's message. Paul's message had been "to the Jew first, and also to the Greek" (Rom. 1:16), but now he decides to stop going to the Jew first. Now Paul brings the message of how God solved the sin problem with His powerful loving sacrifice to the Gentiles.**</u>

<u>**During this dispensation of the grace of God, only those who believe the gospel of Christ (1 Cor. 15:1-4) become members of the body of Christ.**</u>

God's Secret

It is important when studying the Bible <u>NOT to claim our neighbor's mail</u>. All scripture is profitable for our learning. But we need to know who God is speaking to. Some instruction in the Bible is for past saints and some for future Israel that does not have anything to do with the Church today.

The Mystery

<u>In the Bible, a mystery is a divine secret kept by God until He decides to reveal it. Many people today believe that Paul's ministry merely involved the salvation of the Gentiles, but it was much more than that.</u> Paul preached the Mystery: that God was forming a <u>new agency</u>, the body of Christ, <u>to populate and fill the heavenly places</u>. The Church will replace and judge the evil angels.

The dispensation of grace in which we live is called a "mystery" because it was not prophesied but was revealed by Christ to Paul and then to us.

Perhaps the greatest exposition on the Grace message found in the Bible are the following verses (read them slowly several times). "For this cause <u>I Paul</u>, the prisoner of Jesus Christ for you Gentiles, If ye have heard of the <u>DISPENSATION OF THE GRACE OF GOD</u> which is <u>GIVEN ME TO YOU-WARD</u>: How that <u>by revelation he made known unto me the mystery</u>;

(as I wrote afore in few words, Whereby, when ye READ, ye may UNDERSTAND MY KNOWLEDGE in the <u>MYSTERY</u> of Christ)

Which <u>IN OTHER AGES WAS NOT MADE KNOWN UNTO THE SONS OF MEN</u>, as it is <u>NOW REVEALED</u> unto his holy apostles and prophets by the Spirit; That the <u>GENTILES</u> should be <u>FELLOWHEIRS</u>, and <u>OF THE SAME BODY</u>, and <u>PARTAKERS OF HIS PROMISE IN CHRIST BY THE GOSPEL</u>: Whereof <u>I was MADE A MINISTER</u>, according to the <u>GIFT OF</u>

A Primer with Pictures for How to Rightly Divide the Word of Truth

THE GRACE OF GOD GIVEN UNTO ME by the **EFFECTUAL WORKING OF HIS POWER**. Unto **ME**, who am less than the least of all saints, is this **GRACE GIVEN**, that I should **PREACH** among the Gentiles the **UNSEARCHABLE** [not found in Scripture before] **RICHES** of Christ; And to make **ALL MEN SEE** what *is* the **FELLOWSHIP OF THE MYSTERY**, which FROM THE BEGINNING OF THE WORLD HATH BEEN **HID IN GOD**, WHO CREATED ALL THINGS BY JESUS CHRIST" (Eph. 3:1-9).

We now know what this Mystery was, and so does Satan. "To the intent that NOW unto the principalities and powers in heavenly *places* might be known by the church THE MANIFOLD WISDOM OF GOD" (Eph. 3:10).

God's wisdom has been made known, and the principalities and powers are learning what God has done and is doing through the body of Christ believers.

DUE TIME

Why did the dispensation of grace not begin at the cross? Because it was not yet "due time." The SECRET God had kept was revealed to Paul precisely at the right time, in "due time." It was NOT due time during the earthly ministry of Jesus Christ. It was NOT due time during Israel's one-year extension of mercy. But when Israel rejected the third Person of the Godhead, the Holy Ghost, by stoning Stephen, then it was due time. Without warning the Lord Jesus Christ from heaven dramatically saved Paul (no one else has ever been saved that way), and made him His Apostle to "all nations" (Rom. 1:5 and 16:26). (Israel fell down to the level of all other nations.)

God's Secret

It was NOW due time for God to reveal the glorious SECRET which He had kept to Paul so that Paul could write about it. "But hath in **DUE TIMES** manifested his word through **preaching, which is COMMITTED UNTO ME** according to the COMMANDMENT of God our Saviour" (Titus 1:3).

To Paul Jesus revealed that He had not only died for Israel but for the Gentiles also. "Who gave himself a **ransom for all, to be testified** in **due time**" (1 Tim. 2:6). "For when we were yet without strength, in **due time** Christ died for the ungodly" (Rom. 5:6).

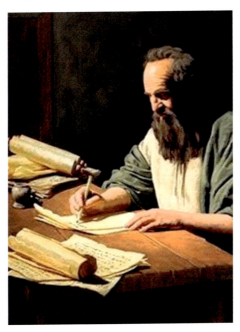

What was the SECRET?

God revealed to Paul that He was **holding back His week of wrath**, and temporarily suspending His prophetic program with Israel and that He was **bringing in a new and un-prophesied dispensation**. God is NOW reclaiming the **dominion** of heaven from "the prince of the power of the air," Satan.

God also revealed to Paul that He was **forming a new agency** the "one new man" (Eph. 2:15) the Church, the body of Christ, to fill the heavenly places. "And hath raised us up together, and made us sit together **in heavenly places** in Christ Jesus" (Eph. 2:6).

This new agency, the body of Christ, **is the secret**. It is made up of both individual Jews and Gentiles. "**That the Gentiles should be fellowheirs [with the individual Jews, not the nation], and of the same body, and partakers of his promise in Christ by the gospel**" (Eph. 3:6).

Sound Doctrine

Paul encouraged Titus, his fellow worker in the ministry to hold fast to the sound doctrine revealed to him. "Holding fast the faithful word as he hath been taught, that he may be able by <u>sound doctrine</u> both to exhort and to convince the gainsayers" (Titus 1:9).

Paul said that he did not receive <u>his information</u> from another human but from Jesus Christ. "But I certify you brethren, that the gospel which was preached of me is not after man. <u>For I neither received it of man</u>, neither was I taught *it*, <u>but by the revelation of Jesus Christ</u>" (Gal. 1:11, 12).

The information or <u>sound doctrine</u>, given to Paul from the ascended Lord Jesus is found in his 13 letters, Romans to Philemon. Second Timothy was the last book written in the Bible. "Whereof I am made a minister, according to the dispensation of God which is given to me for you, to <u>FULFIL THE WORD OF GOD</u>; Even the <u>MYSTERY</u> which has been <u>HID FROM AGES</u> and from generations, but <u>NOW</u> is made <u>MANIFEST to his saints</u>" (Col. 1:25, 26).

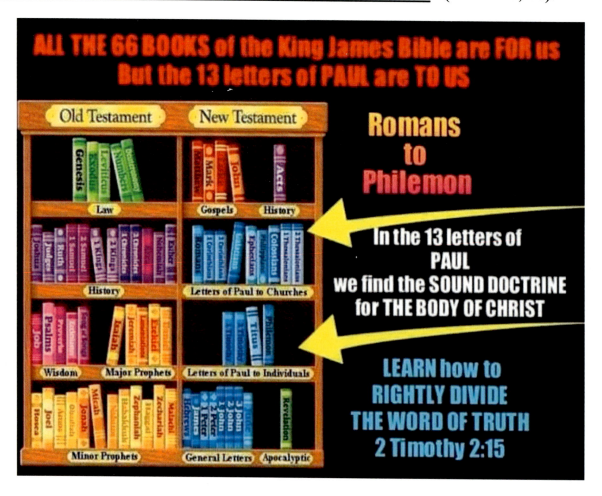

God's Secret

My Gospel

The ascended Lord Jesus Christ made Paul the Apostle of the Gentiles and gave him a distinctive ministry. Three times Paul says MY Gospel:

1. Paul says that Jesus Christ will judge unbelievers in this dispensation by his gospel. "In the day when God shall JUDGE the secrets of men by Jesus Christ according to MY GOSPEL" (Rom. 2:16).

2. Believers today can be established according to the gospel and the preaching of Jesus Christ, according to the revelation of the mystery kept secret since the world began, but that is now made known. "Now to him that is of power to stablish you according to MY GOSPEL, and the preaching of Jesus Christ, according to the revelation of the mystery, which was kept secret since the world began, but now is made manifest . . ." (Rom. 16:25, 26).

3. Jesus Christ, of the lineage of David, rose according to Paul's gospel. "Remember that Jesus Christ of the SEED of David was raised from the dead according to MY GOSPEL" (2 Tim. 2:8).

Paul says "my gospel" because Christ gave the revelation to him.

Paul explained how God solved the sin problem of mankind with imputed righteousness. "Now it was not written for his sake alone, that it was imputed to him; But for us also, to whom it shall be imputed, if we believe on him that raised up Jesus our Lord from the dead; Who was delivered for our offences, and was raised again for our justification" (Rom. 4:23-25).

Paul revealed how God could remain just while declaring a believing sinner justified because of Christ's fully satisfying blood sacrifice as payment for sins, and His imputed righteousness. "Being justified freely by his grace through the redemption that is in Christ Jesus: Whom God hath set forth *to be* a propitiation through faith in his blood, to declare his righteousness for the remission of sins that are past, through the forbearance of God; To declare, *I* [Paul] *say*, at this time his righteousness: that he might be just, and the justifier of him which believeth in Jesus" (Rom. 3:24-26).

From heaven, the Lord Jesus Christ gave a distinctive message and ministry to Paul for the body of Christ in this dispensation. "For if I do this thing willingly, I have a reward: but if against my will, a dispensation of the gospel is committed unto me" (1 Cor. 9:17).

A Primer with Pictures for How to Rightly Divide the Word of Truth

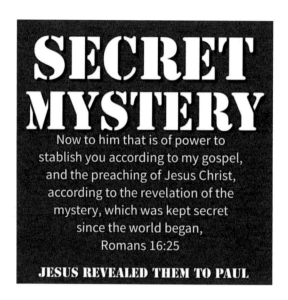

THE SECRET

God had a SECRET, but it is now revealed. God had kept His plan of the formation of the body of Christ in the dispensation of grace a mystery (unknown since before the foundation of the earth). "According as he hath CHOSEN US IN HIM BEFORE THE FOUNDATION OF THE WORLD, that we should be holy and without blame before him in love" (Eph. 1:4).

God revealed His SECRET to all through Paul. Paul explains that he was given the secret of the mystery. "*Even* the mystery which hath been hid from ages and from generations, but now is made manifest to his saints" (Col. 1:26). "Now to him that is of power to stablish you according to my gospel, and the preaching of Jesus Christ, according to the revelation of the MYSTERY, which was kept SECRET since the world began, BUT NOW IS MADE MANIFEST. . ." (Rom. 16:25, 26). A mystery is hidden wisdom (information).

God said that Satan thought that he was "wiser than Daniel; there is no secret that they can hide from thee" (Ezek. 28:3). But Satan was wrong, there was a secret "hid in God" (Eph. 3:9) that he didn't know. God inserted the mystery, the dispensation of grace, between the 69th and 70th week of Daniel's timeline.

The SECRET is out, so now the goal for the Church is to help everyone know it because Satan still wants to conceal it. "And to MAKE ALL MEN SEE what is the fellowship of the mystery, which from the beginning of the world hath been HID IN GOD, who created all things by Jesus Christ" (Eph. 3:9).

"It is the glory of God to conceal a thing [keep a secret]" (Proverbs 25:2).

God's Secret

Why did God Keep This Secret?

God kept the secret so that Satan would not know that God's goal was to reclaim both the Heaven and the Earth and that Christ would triumph on the cross. Because Satan would NOT have allowed Christ to be crucified if he knew that God planned to reclaim not only the Earth but also the Heaven. "But we speak the <u>WISDOM OF GOD IN A MYSTERY</u>, *even* the <u>*HIDDEN WISDOM*</u>, which <u>GOD ORDAINED BEFORE THE WORLD UNTO OUR GLORY</u>: Which <u>NONE of the PRINCES of THIS WORLD</u> [Satan, his cohorts, and people empowered by him] <u>KNEW</u>: for <u>HAD THEY KNOWN IT</u>, they would <u>NOT have CRUCIFIED the LORD of GLORY</u>" (1 Cor. 2:7, 8).

<u>God caught Satan in his own craftiness</u>.
Satan thought he had destroyed God's plan when Christ was rejected by His people and crucified. But the crucifixion sealed Satan's doom. "For the wisdom of this world is foolishness with God. For it is written, He taketh the wise [Satan] in their <u>own craftiness</u>" (1 Cor. 3:19).

God's wisdom was to keep the secret from being published in His word because Satan reads the Bible and then tries to foil God's plan. Satan brought about His own defeat when he crucified Christ and lost everything.

At Calvary Jesus Christ was victorious over Satan and the fallen angels. "*And having spoiled* [plundered, robbed] *principalities and powers* [the temporary governmental domains of Satan and his cohorts], *he made a shew of them openly,* <u>TRIUMPHING</u> *over them in it*" (Col. 2:15).

The secret is revealed. "Which in <u>OTHER AGES WAS NOT MADE KNOWN UNTO THE SONS OF MEN</u>, as it is <u>NOW REVEALED</u> . . . which <u>FROM THE BEGINNING OF THE WORLD HATH BEEN HID IN GOD</u>, who created all things by Jesus Christ" (Eph. 3:5, 9).

<u>Satan could NOT trace the plan to build the heavenly body of Christ</u> in the Bible because <u>it was not revealed anywhere in the Bible</u> until it was revealed to Paul. "O the depth of the riches both of the wisdom and knowledge of God! how <u>UNSEARCHABLE</u> [the dispensation of grace and the formation of the body of Christ were untraceable until God revealed them through Paul] *are* his judgments, and his ways past finding out!" (Rom. 11:33).

<u>God proved that He is "the only wise God" (1 Tim. 1:17)</u>. God outsmarted the wisest being that He had created, and used the Devil (Satan) for His purposes.

A Primer with Pictures for How to Rightly Divide the Word of Truth

The Key Verse in the Bible:

The only verse in the Bible that tells us how to study the Bible is <u>2 Tim. 2:15</u>: "<u>Study</u> to shew thyself approved unto God, a workman that needeth not to be ashamed, <u>RIGHTLY DIVIDING THE WORD OF TRUTH</u>."

The instruction is to divide truth. Not error from truth, but truth from truth. All the Bible is truth, but it needs to be divided up so we know which part is our truth. It makes sense that Paul who told us to divide truth, would also tell us how to divide truth, and he does in Ephesians chapter two.

In Ephesians chapter two Paul gives us three time divisions: <u>Time Past, But Now, Ages to Come</u>

<u>Time Past</u>: Eph. 2:11, 12 Wherefore remember, that ye *being* in TIME PAST Gentiles in the flesh, who are called Uncircumcision by that which is called the Circumcision in the flesh made by hands; That at that time ye were without Christ, being aliens from the commonwealth of Israel, and strangers from the covenants of promise, having no hope, and without God in the world.

<u>But Now</u>: Eph. 2:13 BUT NOW in Christ Jesus ye who sometimes were far off are made nigh by the blood of Christ.

<u>Ages to Come</u>: Eph. 2:7 That in the AGES TO COME he might shew the exceeding riches of his grace in *his* kindness toward us through Christ Jesus.

Jesus Christ revealed to us through Paul how to divide the word of God.

A distinctive feature indicating that <u>Time Past</u> is in effect is whenever God makes a distinction between the Jews and all other nations. This distinction is called "<u>the middle wall of partition</u>" (Eph. 2:14). God gave Israel the covenant of circumcision (Gen. 17) making them unlike all other nations. When God added the law by Moses He solidified the difference between the Jews and Gentiles even more through dietary, and other laws. In fact, Israel was given a total of 613 laws by God. The nation of Israel was "born" out of Egypt. He set the nation of Israel (the circumcision) above the rest of the nations. Whenever the word of God distinguishes between Jews and Gentiles we know that "prophecy" not "mystery" is in effect. (In the <u>Ages to Come</u> (prophecy) the law, and Israel's preferred nation status will again be in effect.)

Today we are living in the <u>But Now</u>, the dispensation of grace. We are NOT living under the law today. Currently, we are saved apart from Israel, and

apart from the law, there is no difference between a Gentile and a Jew today. Israel as a nation is not worshiping their Messiah at this time, they do not have preferred nation status at this time. They only occupy a small sliver of all the land promised to them. Paul received "the gospel of the grace of God" (Acts 20:24), from the ascended Lord Jesus Christ and preached "the gospel of Christ" (Rom. 1:16) the power of God to salvation to all who would believe.

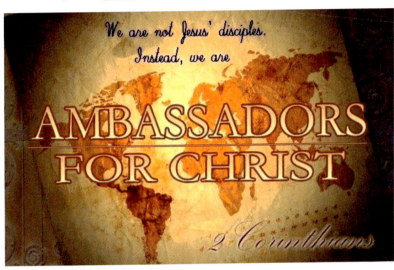

New Creatures, Ambassadors

Believers in the gospel (1 Cor. 15:1-4) become new creatures in Christ individually when they trust what Jesus has done and also become part of the new creature, the Church, the body of Christ. As believers, we are not the same person we used to be. The "old" us died when we identified with Christ's death on the cross, and His resurrection. We are new creatures, with new natures in a new dispensation, in a new agency with a new destiny. "Therefore if any man be in Christ, he is a new creature: old things are passed away; behold, all things have become new" (2 Cor. 5:17). Thank You, Lord!

As believers, we have been given the ministry of reconciliation to help others to trust what Jesus has done and to be reconciled to God. Through Christ "we have peace with God" (Rom. 5:1), and we are to tell others how they can have this peace. ". . . God, who hath reconciled us to himself by Jesus Christ, and hath given to us the ministry of reconciliation; . . . that God was in Christ, reconciling the world unto himself, NOT IMPUTING their trespasses unto them; and hath committed unto us the word of reconciliation. Now then we are AMBASSADORS FOR CHRIST, as though God did beseech [beg] you by us: we pray you in Christ's stead [in His place], be ye reconciled [from being enemies to being friends by faith] to God" (2 Cor. 5:18-20).

A Primer with Pictures for How to Rightly Divide the Word of Truth

God is dispensing grace today, not imputing sins. It is unbelief, not sins which keep a person from having eternal life with God. Believers are part of this ministry. We are ambassadors because we are already seated with Christ in heaven. "And hath raised us up together, and made us sit together in heavenly places in Christ Jesus" (Eph. 2:6).

Like all foreign Ambassadors, the body of Christ believers will be called home (Raptured) before the war (the Wrath of God). We do this ministry because of our love for Christ, not because we have to, but want to. He loved us. "For the LOVE OF CHRIST constraineth us . . ." (2 Cor. 5:14).

What is Satan's Policy of Evil in this Dispensation?

Satan blinds the minds of those who are lost from the glorious gospel. "But if our gospel be hid, it is hid to them that are lost: In whom the god of this world hath blinded the minds of them which believe not, lest the light of the glorious gospel of Christ, who is the image of God, should shine on them" (2 Cor. 4:3, 4). Sound doctrine is our defense against false doctrine.

Satan also attacks the message, the messenger, discredits the messenger, discourages the messenger, and tries to bring division between the body of Christ believers.

Christ did not reveal the fact that it was checkmate at the cross to Satan until Paul. Not only did "the god of this world" (2 Cor. 4:4) lose the Earth, but the "prince of the power of the air" (Eph. 2:2) realized that he lost the Heavenly Places also when he heard the mystery. God won by simply keeping a secret.

Today Satan is causing as much trouble as he can, especially in the churches. There is only one true Church, the body of Christ, yet today we have so many denominations, because of the doctrines of men. Satan is happy when pastors teach that believers are "spiritual Israel" (mixing the things that belong to Israel, with those that belong to the Church), mix law and grace, and add works such as water baptism, speaking in tongues, and other requirements as necessary for salvation. "And no marvel; for Satan himself is transformed into an angel of light" (2 Cor. 11:14).

Satan is creating corrupt Bibles which hide the truth of the word of God rightly divided, and the mystery of the formation of the body of Christ.

But we are secure in Christ ". . . your life is hid with Christ in God" (Col. 3:3).

God's Secret

God's Twofold Will for Today

Once we realize God's twofold will, we do our best, to do our part. "Who WILL have ALL MEN to be SAVED, and to come unto the KNOWLEDGE OF THE TRUTH" (1 Tim. 2:4).

Faith NOT Works

We are saved by grace through faith in what Jesus has done, NOT by our works. There will be No boasting in heaven. "For <u>by grace</u> ye are saved <u>through faith</u> [in the salvation accomplished by Christ]; and that not of yourselves: *it is* the gift of God: <u>NOT of WORKS, lest any man should boast</u>" (Eph. 2:8, 9). Once we are saved we can do good works out of love for God.

No Sign Gifts Today

The body of Christ believers do not follow physical signs. We walk in the spirit, not in the flesh. We "live by faith" (Rom. 1:17). Faith is believing what God says in His word. We <u>build up the inward man</u> (soul and spirit) by understanding the <u>sound doctrine</u> given to us by God through Paul. After arriving in Rome on house arrest Paul set the Jews aside in Acts 28:28, and healing died out. God told Paul "my grace is sufficient for thee: for my strength is made perfect in weakness" (2 Cor. 12:9). Later Paul left his friend sick because he could not heal him. ". . . Trophimus have I left at Miletum sick" (2 Tim. 4:20). The Body of Christ believers "walk by faith, not by sight" (2 Cor. 5:7). In the present dispensation of grace, God is more interested in building up our inner man (soul and spirit) through His word. When we go to heaven our inner man is all that we can take with us.

No Physical Circumcision

Our circumcision is spiritual, not physical. The removal of a little piece of skin does not matter. What matters is what Christ has done for us on the cross. "In whom also ye are circumcised with the CIRCUMCISION made WITHOUT HANDS, in putting off the body of the sins of the flesh by the circumcision of Christ" (Col. 2:11). He removed the consequences of sin from the believer, He cut off the power of sin, and at the rapture, He will free us from the presence of sin. "Who delivered us from so great a death, and doth deliver: in whom we trust that he will yet deliver us" (2 Cor. 1:13).

We are saved by "the hearing of faith" (Gal. 3:2) in what Christ has DONE, NOT made perfect in our flesh. We walk by faith in God's word so that by love we can serve one another. "For in Jesus Christ neither circumcision availeth any thing, nor uncircumcision; but faith which worketh by love" (Gal. 5:6). Faith in the finished work of Christ is what matters.

Our Baptism Is Spiritual, Not Physical

Today there is only one baptism, "One Lord, one faith, one baptism, . . ." (Eph. 4:5) and it is spiritual, not physical. We are baptized into the body of Christ which does not involve a drop of water. "For by one Spirit are we ALL baptized into one body, whether *we be* JEWS or GENTILES, whether *we be* bond or free; and have been all made to drink into one Spirit" (1 Cor. 12:13).

Paul said that Christ sent him NOT to baptize. In contrast, Peter said water baptism was necessary to demonstrate one's faith in Christ. Paul preached Christ crucified, and risen again (the offence of the cross). "For Christ sent me NOT TO BAPTIZE, but to preach the gospel: not with wisdom of words, lest the cross of Christ should be made of none effect. For the preaching of the cross is to them that perish foolishness; but unto us which are saved it is the power of God" (1 Cor. 1:17, 18).

Peter taught water baptism because Israel was to be a holy nation of washed kingdom priests. But Paul said that our baptism is "identification" with the death, burial and resurrection of Jesus Christ. "Know ye not, that so many of us as were baptized into Jesus Christ were baptized into HIS DEATH? Therefore we are buried with him by baptism into death [NO WATER]: that like as Christ was raised up from the dead by the glory of the Father, even so we also should walk in NEWNESS OF LIFE" (Rom. 6:3, 4).

God's Secret

The believer is baptized into Christ and becomes a member of the body of Christ. Spiritual baptism is something God does, not the believer.

Believers have Christ's righteousness - our sins were judged at the cross. Our old nature was crucified, and we are raised with Him having a new nature.

Paul worked to lay the foundation of the Church. Clearly, <u>Paul suffered many things for the Church, the body of Christ's sake</u>. Toward the end of his life, he wrote to Timothy to say that almost everyone had abandoned him, but that he knew that the Lord would be able to keep what he had committed unto him. "For the which cause I also suffer these things: nevertheless I am not ashamed: <u>for I know whom I have believed, and am persuaded that he is able to keep that which I have committed unto him against that day</u>" (2 Tim. 1:12).

If you are understanding the message of grace given in the Bible and explained in this book, then it proves that the Lord has been faithful.

The letters of Paul follow the order given in 2 Tim. 3:16 <u>All scripture *is* given by inspiration of God</u>, and *is* profitable for DOCTRINE, for REPROOF, for CORRECTION, for INSTRUCTION IN RIGHTEOUSNESS:

Romans = doctrine
1 & 2 Corinthians = reproof
Galatians = correction
Ephesians = doctrine
Philippians = reproof
Colossians = correction
1 & 2 Thessalonians = doctrine, instruction in righteousness
1 & 2 Timothy, Titus, Philemon = doctrine, instruction in righteousness

Paul said that if we understand the "sound doctrine" in his letters, then we would be able to understand the rest of the Bible. "<u>CONSIDER what I SAY; and the LORD give thee UNDERSTANDING in ALL THINGS</u>" (2 Tim. 2:7).

The Father of our Lord Jesus Christ ". . . hath put all things under his feet, and gave him to be the HEAD [Christ] over all things to the CHURCH, Which is HIS BODY, the fulness of him that filleth all in all" (Eph. 1:22, 23).

The rapture of the Church was not revealed until Jesus revealed it to Paul. The rapture is a mystery exclusively found in Paul's epistles.

The Rapture

The rapture is the next event in God's plan, do NOT miss being part of it.

It will be swift. The vile body is changed. "Behold, I shew you <u>a mystery</u>; We shall not all sleep, but we <u>shall all be changed, In a moment, in the twinkling of an eye</u>, at the last trump: for the trumpet shall sound, and the dead shall be raised <u>incorruptible</u>, and we shall be changed" (1 Cor. 15:51, 52).

We have a blessed hope. "Looking for that <u>blessed hope</u>, and the glorious appearing of the great God and our Saviour Jesus Christ" (Titus 2:13).

The body of Christ will be caught up to meet the Lord in the air, and the dispensation of the grace of God will end. "For the Lord himself shall descend from heaven with a shout, with the voice of the archangel, and with the trump of God: and the <u>dead in Christ shall rise first</u>: Then <u>we which are alive</u> and remain shall be <u>caught up</u> together with them in the clouds, to <u>meet the Lord in the air</u>: and so shall we ever be with the Lord" (1 Thess. 4:16, 17).

Heaven is the destination for the body of Christ, not the earth. Therefore, "Set your affection on <u>things above</u>, not on things on the earth" (Col. 3:2).

Next is the "judgment seat of Christ" (2 Corinthians 5:10) where we will be judged for service done "in *his* body . . . whether *it* be good or bad." After that, we will "appear with him in glory" (Colossians 3:4).

FUTURE
Hebrews to Revelation

Hebrews through Revelation is the portion of scripture dealing with the resumption of God's program with Israel. The Hebrew people are once again God's special preferred nation and <u>the middle wall of partition</u> will be back up. Believers will use all of the Bible, but these books will especially help them to navigate through the Tribulation and enter the kingdom. Following Paul to follow Christ will no longer be the correct thing to do (1 Cor. 11:1).

The rapture is over, and so is the chance of joining the body of Christ. The dispensation of the grace of God has ended. The Law has resumed.

Even at the end of the dispensation of grace many people will "depart from the faith" and fall away from Pauline truth. "Now the Spirit speaketh expressly, that in the latter times some shall DEPART FROM THE FAITH, giving heed to seducing spirits, and doctrines of devils" (1 Tim. 4:1).

There is more than one mystery in the Bible. The Mystery of Iniquity was already in operation in Paul's day; actually it was at work since the time that iniquity was found in Lucifer/Satan when he was in heaven with God (Ezek. 28:15). "For the mystery of iniquity doth already work . . ." (2 Thess. 2:7).

The Gentiles still on earth will have hope if they believe in Israel's Messiah and bless Israel, as mentioned in Matthew chapter 25:31-40.

Meanwhile, in heaven God has more wonders in store for the body of Christ believers. "That in the <u>**AGES TO COME**</u> he might shew the exceeding riches of his grace in his kindness toward us through Christ Jesus" (Ephesians 2:7).

KINGDOM ESTABLISHED

ALL believing Israel are to be saved. When the fullness of the Gentiles is come in with the Rapture, then shall ALL believing Israel be saved. "For I would not, brethren, that ye should be ignorant of this mystery, lest ye should be wise in your own conceits; that blindness in part is happened to Israel, UNTIL THE <u>FULNESS OF THE GENTILES BE COME IN</u>. And so ALL ISRAEL SHALL BE SAVED: as it is written, There SHALL COME OUT OF SION THE DELIVERER, and SHALL TURN AWAY UNGODLINESS FROM JACOB" (Rom. 11:25, 26).

Comparing Israel with the Body of Christ

Israel	Body of Christ
• Gospel of Kingdom • Earthly Promises, hopes and blessings • Christ is King • Physical • National Salvation • 12 Apostles • Under Law • Water Baptism • Christ's return to earth	• Gospel of the grace of God • Heavenly promises, hopes and blessings • Christ is Head • Spiritual • Individual Salvation • 1 Apostle • Under Grace • Spirit Baptism • Christ's meeting in the air

The Tribulation will be the last chance to believe God and enter the kingdom. Simeon prophesied the fall and rising again of Israel. "And Simeon blessed them, and said unto Mary his mother, Behold, <u>this child is set for the fall and rising again of many in Israel</u>" (Luke 2:34).

God's Secret

The Tribulation

The Tribulation (the 70th week of Daniel) begins when Antichrist signs the seven-year covenant with Israel to allow animal sacrifices to be made in the temple at Jerusalem. Daniel's prophecy: "And after threescore and two weeks shall Messiah be cut off [die on the cross], but not for himself [for Israel, and all mankind]: and the people of the prince [Antichrist] that shall come shall destroy the city and the sanctuary; and the end thereof *shall be* with a flood, and unto the end of the war desolations are determined [Tribulation]. And he [Antichrist] shall confirm the <u>covenant with many</u> [Israel] for ONE WEEK [seven years]: and in the midst of the week he shall cause the sacrifice and the oblation to cease [stop the sacrifices after 3 ½ years], and for the overspreading of abominations he shall make *it* desolate [set himself up as the "christ"], even until the consummation, and that determined shall be poured upon the desolate [end of the great Tribulation]" (Dan. 9:26, 27).

The Tribulation ("Jacob's trouble" Jer. 30:7) is a dreadful time with God sending strong delusion on the people so they will believe a lie. The wrong christ rules. The lie is that Antichrist is god, and that people can be like little gods (like the first lie believed by Satan and Eve) ". . . they received not the love of the truth, that they might be saved. And for this cause God shall send them strong delusion, that they should believe <u>a lie</u>" (2 Thess. 2:10, 11).

God will send judgments with increasing severity on Israel and the world: seven seals, seven trumpets, and seven vials of plagues, to get people to turn to Him. In the middle of the wrath, Michael and his angels will fight against Satan and his angels and win. "<u>Satan . . . was cast out into the earth, and his angels were cast out with him</u> . . . rejoice *ye* heavens, and ye that dwell in

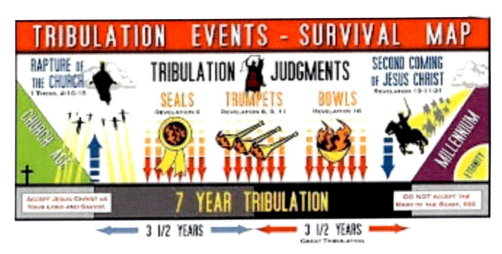

them. Woe to the inhabiters of the earth . . . for the devil is come down unto you, having great wrath, because he knoweth that he hath but a short time" (Rev. 12:7-12). God will purge out the rebels from Israel (Ezek. 20:38, 22:21).

People will not be allowed to buy or sell unless they have the Mark of the Beast. Anyone who takes that Mark will NOT enter the kingdom on earth. Believers will not take that Mark. "And that no man might buy or sell, save he that had the MARK, or the name of the beast, or the number of his name . . . his number is Six hundred threescore *and* six [666]" (Rev. 13:17, 18).

People will be evangelized by the 144,000 sealed from the 12 tribes of Israel, and His two witnesses (the resurrected Moses and Elijah, Rev. 11:3). Salvation will be given to those who keep the faith in the Tribulation. "But he that shall endure unto the end, the same shall be saved" (Matt. 24:13).

Christ's Second Coming

Watch therefore: for ye know not what hour your Lord doth come (Matt 24:42)

After the Tribulation is the Second Coming of Jesus to earth. He will put down all opposition at the battle of Armageddon and elsewhere with the word of His mouth. "And I saw heaven opened, and behold a white horse; and he that sat upon him was called Faithful and True, and in righteousness he doth judge and make war . . . The Word of God . . . KING OF KINGS, AND LORD OF LORDS" (Rev. 19:11, 13, 16).

Many believers will be kept in a protected place during the Tribulation. When they see Christ coming they will look at Him, believe and mourn. "And I will pour upon the house of David, and upon the inhabitants of Jerusalem, the spirit of grace and of supplications: and THEY SHALL LOOK UPON ME WHOM THEY HAVE PIERCED, and they shall mourn for him, AS ONE MOURNETH FOR HIS ONLY SON, and shall be in bitterness for him, as one that is in bitterness for *his* firstborn" (Zech. 12:10).

The unbelievers of Israel are removed at "the harvest" (the tares Matt. 13:24-30) but those Gentiles who have shown that they believe in Jesus the Messiah by **blessing Israel** with food, shelter, clothing, and other needs will be saved.

Jesus will separate the Gentile sheep (believers) from the Gentile goats (unbelievers) of all the nations of the world based on the Abrahamic covenant (bless and curse, Gen. 12:1-3) and the sheep will enter into the kingdom "then shall he sit upon the throne of his glory . . . And before him shall be gathered all nations: and he shall separate them one from another, as a shepherd divideth HIS SHEEP FROM THE GOATS: Then shall the King say unto them [the sheep] on his right hand, come, ye blessed of my father, inherit the KINGDOM PREPARED FOR YOU FROM THE FOUNDATION OF THE WORLD: For I was an hungered, and ye gave me meat [food]: I was thirsty, and ye gave me drink: I was a stranger, and ye took me in" (Matt. 25:31-35).

The beast (Antichrist) and the false prophet will be cast alive into the lake of fire and all their people will be slain by the word of God. "And the BEAST was taken, and with him the FALSE PROPHET that wrought miracles before him, with which he deceived them that had received the MARK OF THE BEAST, and them that worshipped his image. These both were CAST ALIVE INTO THE LAKE OF FIRE burning with brimstone" (Rev. 19:20).

What Will Happen to Satan?

Satan is cast into the bottomless pit for one thousand years ". . . AN ANGEL . . . from heaven, having the key of the bottomless pit and a great chain in his hand . . . laid hold on the dragon, that old serpent, which is the Devil, and Satan, and **bound him a thousand years, And cast him into the bottomless pit, and shut him up, and set a seal upon him, that he should deceive the nations no more, till the thousand years should be fulfilled:** and AFTER THAT HE MUST BE LOOSED FOR A SEASON" (Rev. 20:1-3).

A Primer with Pictures for How to Rightly Divide the Word of Truth

The Millennial Reign of Christ

The prayer "Thy kingdom come" (Matt. 6:10) will be realized when Jesus Christ sets up His physical kingdom and fills it with the resurrected kingdom on earth believers and the Tribulation saints who stayed true to the LORD and His word. "And I saw thrones, and they sat upon them, and judgment was given unto them: and I saw the souls of them that were beheaded for the witness of Jesus, and for the word of God, and which had not worshipped the beast, neither his image, neither had received his mark upon their foreheads, or in their hands; and they lived and reigned with Christ a thousand years" (Rev. 20:4).

Jesus will be the King of the Jews and will establish His kingdom on this earth for a thousand years ". . . they shall be priests of God and of Christ, and shall reign with him a thousand years" (Rev. 20:6).

Israel will rise, be a shining example and a CHANNEL OF BLESSING "the Gentiles shall come to thy light, and kings to the brightness of thy rising" (Isa. 60:3). Israel will be a kingdom of priests. "But ye shall be named the Priests of the LORD . . . the Ministers of our God" (Isaiah 61:6).

The millennial reign of Christ will be a time of a peaceful, one world monarchy, the LORD will teach the nations His word, and the kingdom of priests will help. The Gentiles will be blessed through Israel, ". . . And it shall come to pass in the last days, that the LORD'S house shall be established in the top of the mountains, . . . and all nations shall flow unto it. And many people shall go and say, Come ye, and LET US GO UP TO . . . the house of the GOD of JACOB; and he will teach us of HIS WAYS, and we will walk in his paths: for out of Zion shall go forth the law, and the WORD of the LORD from JERUSALEM. And he shall judge among the nations, . . . neither shall they learn war any more" (Isaiah 2:2-4).

The people of Israel will be perfectly healed so they can minister as priests, "the eyes of the blind will be opened, the ears of the deaf shall be unstopped; Then shall the lame *man* leap as an hart [deer] . . ." (Isaiah 35:5, 6).

In the kingdom, Christ will lift the curse and restore the earth. The time of refreshing which Peter told the men of Israel about will have come (Acts 3:19-21) because the earth will be restored to what it was like in the beginning when Adam and Eve were in the Garden of Eden (Ezek. 36:35).

God's Secret

Israelites will need the gift of tongues (languages) at this time as **they teach the nations about the LORD.** "Yea, many people and strong nations shall come to seek the LORD of hosts in Jerusalem . . . it shall come to pass, that **ten men shall take hold out of all languages of the nations,** even **shall take hold of the skirt of him that is a Jew,** saying, we will go with you: for we have heard *that* GOD *IS* WITH YOU" (Zech. 8:22, 23).

The promises and covenants will be fulfilled. Israel will have the **land, seed, and blessing forever. All kingdom believers will be raised up from their graves and enter the kingdom** ". . . and shall sit down with Abraham, and Isaac, and Jacob, in the kingdom of heaven" (Matt. 8:11).

David will be raised to rule with Christ ". . . **they shall serve the LORD their God, and David their king, whom I will raise up unto them**" (Jer. 30:9).

The twelve Apostles will rule with Jesus (Luke 22:28-30). **Jesus the King will reign over Israel forever.** "And **he shall reign over the house of Jacob for ever; and of his kingdom there shall be no end**" (Luke 1:33).

God takes back the kingdoms from Satan (Rev. 11:15). Christ will rule with a rod of iron (Rev. 19:15) and **all the world will know Him.** "And they shall not teach every man his neighbour, and every man his brother, saying, Know the Lord: for **all shall know me,** from the least to the greatest" (Hebrews 8:11).

God will put His New Covenant in the hearts and minds of the believers of Israel and **cause them to walk in His ways** (Jer. 31:31-34; Ezek. 36:26, 27).

Satan Loosed

After Christ's 1,000-year reign, Satan will be loosed for a season to remove any rebels. A quarter of the Gentiles in the four quarters of the earth will rebel and surround Jerusalem. Some will side with the devil, but most will side with God. Jesus will destroy the opposition (the Devil and his forces who battle against God) with fire from heaven. "And when the THOUSAND YEARS ARE EXPIRED, SATAN shall be LOOSED out of his prison, And SHALL GO OUT to DECEIVE the NATIONS which are in the four quarters of the earth, Gog and Magog, to gather them together to battle: the number of whom is as the sand of the sea . . . and compassed the camp of the saints about, and the beloved city: and **FIRE CAME DOWN FROM GOD OUT OF HEAVEN, AND DEVOURED THEM**" (Rev. 20:7-9).

The Devil is thrown into the Lake of Fire. "And the devil that deceived them was cast into the lake of fire and brimstone, where the beast [Antichrist] and the false prophet are, and shall be tormented day and night for ever and ever" (Rev. 20:10).

The time is up; the opportunity to believe is over ". . . there should be <u>TIME NO LONGER</u>" (Rev. 10:6).

The Great White Throne Judgment

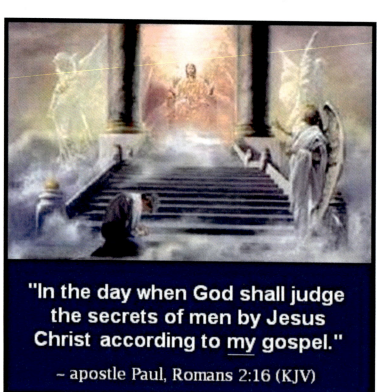

Jesus will judge the lost. The lost who lived in the dispensation of grace will be judged according to Paul's gospel (Rom. 2:16). All unbelievers are cast into the Lake of Fire. "And I saw a GREAT WHITE THRONE, and him that sat on it, from whose face the EARTH AND THE HEAVEN FLED AWAY; and there was found NO PLACE FOR THEM. And I saw the DEAD, SMALL AND GREAT, STAND BEFORE GOD; and the BOOKS were opened: and another book was opened, which is the book of LIFE: and the DEAD WERE JUDGED OUT OF THOSE THINGS WHICH WERE WRITTEN IN THE BOOKS, ACCORDING TO THEIR WORKS. And the SEA GAVE UP the DEAD which were in it; and DEATH and HELL DELIVERED UP THE DEAD which were in them: and they were judged EVERY MAN

ACCORDING TO THEIR WORKS. And DEATH and HELL WERE CAST INTO THE LAKE OF FIRE. THIS IS THE SECOND DEATH. And whosoever was NOT FOUND WRITTEN IN THE BOOK OF LIFE WAS CAST INTO THE LAKE OF FIRE" (Rev. 20:11-15).

New Heaven and New Earth

God will make a new heaven and new earth ". . . I saw a new heaven and a new earth: for the first heaven and the first earth were passed away; and there was no more sea" (Rev. 21:1).

The Dispensation of the Fullness of Times

God will begin the next dispensation of "the fullness of times" (Eph. 1:10) gathering together all true believers in heaven and earth into one.

God's Twofold Plan and Purpose

No one knew about the secret mystery until Jesus Christ revealed it to Paul. The mystery was that God would form the body of Christ believers to rule in the heavenly places. God's twofold plan is to RECLAIM the heaven and the earth, and to POPULATE both places with believers who will willingly love, worship, exalt, and praise Him forever. "Having MADE KNOWN UNTO US THE MYSTERY OF HIS WILL, according to HIS GOOD PLEASURE which he hath PURPOSED IN HIMSELF: That in the DISPENSATION of the FULNESS OF TIMES HE might GATHER together IN ONE ALL THINGS IN CHRIST, both which are in HEAVEN, and which are on EARTH; even in him" (Eph. 1:9, 10). Creation will have been restored.

The Father wagered everything on His Son. The Lord Jesus Christ succeeded in redeeming all mankind. Christ trusted the Father's plan. The cost was very great, the price was His blood, "that he . . . should taste death for every man" (Heb. 2:9). He won the battle and gained the victory. God's plan all along was for Christ to be crucified and resurrected. In Him is eternal life, "I am the resurrection, and the life" (John 11:25). Satan had a plot, but God had a plan.

The conclusion of God's plan: "Then *cometh* the end, when he shall have delivered up the kingdom to God, even the Father . . . the last enemy *that* shall be destroyed *is* death . . . then shall the Son also himself be subject unto him that put all things under him, that God may be all in all" (1 Cor. 15:24-28).

A Primer with Pictures for How to Rightly Divide the Word of Truth

The Kingdom of God
1 Timothy 6:15 KJV

The Lord Jesus Christ is KING and LORD (Rev. 19:16) of both the Heaven and the Earth. "Which in his times he shall shew, who is the <u>blessed and only Potentate, the King of kings, and Lord of lords</u>" (1 Tim. 6:15). The body of Christ will be in ". . . <u>his heavenly kingdom</u> (2 Tim. 4:18). God will have taken <u>dominion</u> as "<u>the most high God, possessor of heaven and earth</u>" (Gen. 14:22).

The kingdom of God has two realms the Heaven and the Earth. In the end, God's plan for mankind and all creation will have worked. He redeemed man, yet allowed him free will, while not compromising His own justice. God redeemed those who put their faith in what God instructed them at that time.

<u>**The greatest story ever told is His-story. Jesus Christ is the Hero. He rescues both His Bride Israel and His Heaven-bound people, the body of Christ, from sin and Satan. Christ won our love and devotion with His loving sacrifice.**</u>

Believers will willingly love and exalt the Lord Jesus Christ, our Redeemer for all eternity, as well as the Father and Holy Spirit who also made our redemption possible. We will join in the glory, of the celebration of love between the Father, Son, and Holy Ghost.

Afterword

I used to be a mixer because I had been taught that the body of Christ began in Acts 2. But once I learned that both the body of Christ and the dispensation of the grace of God both began in Acts 9, I began to understand the Bible better. Contradictions disappeared because it was a matter of understanding different dispensations. Acts 2 is just a continuation of what Christ was doing through His disciples. Matt. 28:18-20 is a commission to preach the "gospel of the kingdom" not the "gospel of Christ." God began something new with Paul, the "mystery" of the body of Christ, kept secret since before the world began.

God says different things to different people at different times. God wrote one thing for the people of Israel and He wrote another thing for us the members of the body of Christ. His goal is to save souls and have fellowship with them. Once I understood the different message to Paul, the mystery of the formation of the body of Christ (to inhabit the heavenly places), I had to unlearn many wrong things which I had learned.

It is NOT enough to be BIBLICAL because it is equally important to be DISPENSATIONAL. To know what is said, who is speaking, to whom he is speaking, when, and what are the prevailing circumstances (the context).

God had a secret which He revealed to Paul, the Apostle of the Gentiles. The Secret is no longer a secret. Paul revealed the secret to all. Now Satan knows that God had kept hidden the fact that Christ would be the Saviour for all, and would form a new agency to fill the heavenly places.

Satan is NOT happy. In Paul's epistles, Satan's demise is clearly found. Not only did "the god of this world" (2 Cor. 4:4) lose the earth, but when Paul revealed the Mystery, the "prince of the power of the air" (Eph. 2:2) realized that he had lost the heavenly places also. God won by simply keeping a secret.

God allowed fallen mankind to have free will and redeemed them while He remained just. He overcame His adversary NOT with power or might but with His incredible wisdom. God is all wise. Christ is the foundation of the kingdom on earth believers according to "prophecy" and the body of Christ believers according to the "mystery." He is the King, the possessor of heaven and earth, and He will populate both places with true believers that love Him.

A Primer with Pictures for How to Rightly Divide the Word of Truth

God's exact word testifies of His genius. In the Bible He ties up all the loose ends. "God is omniscient; therefore, His Word is like a finely woven tapestry from beginning to end" C.R. Stam.

The basic division of the Bible is "prophecy – mystery – prophecy."

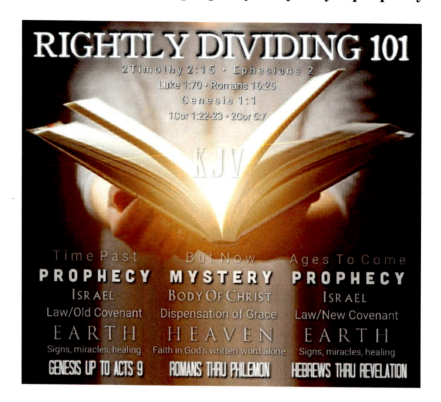

Everything hinges on the true word of God, the KJV. The basic divisions of the Bible are "laid out" in the order of the books of the Bible. All the Bible is truth. The key is to rightly divide truth from truth (2 Tim. 2:15). The word of God is divided into Time Past (Eph. 2:11, 12), But Now (Eph. 2:13), and Ages to Come (Eph. 2:7). God spoke to the <u>kingdom on earth believers</u> by prophets "<u>since the world began</u>" (Luke 1:70). But God gave Paul "the mystery, which was <u>kept secret since the world began</u>" (Rom. 16:25) for the body of Christ, the <u>kingdom in heaven believers</u>. From the beginning, God had a plan for both the Heaven and the Earth (Gen. 1:1). The people of Israel walk by sight (1 Cor. 1:22), but the members of the body of Christ walk by faith (2 Cor. 5:7). We have "all spiritual blessings in heavenly places" (Eph. 1:3).

Christ crucified and risen again is the major foundation for both groups of people. Other people have died on a cruel cross, but only the Lord Jesus Christ resurrected. Jesus is God. Salvation is 100% God, and 0% man.

God's Secret

Appendix

Always remember where you are in God's plan (the dispensation of grace, Eph. 3:2) and what God is doing now (forming the body of Christ).

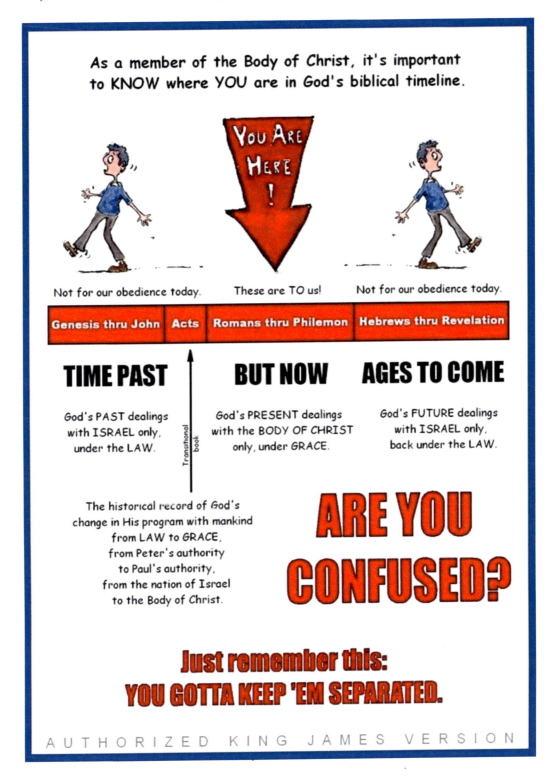

A Primer with Pictures for How to Rightly Divide the Word of Truth

The modern versions (RSV, NIV, NASB, ESV, NLT, NWT, Message, etc.) are all based on Westcott and Hort's corrupt Greek New Testament (1881).

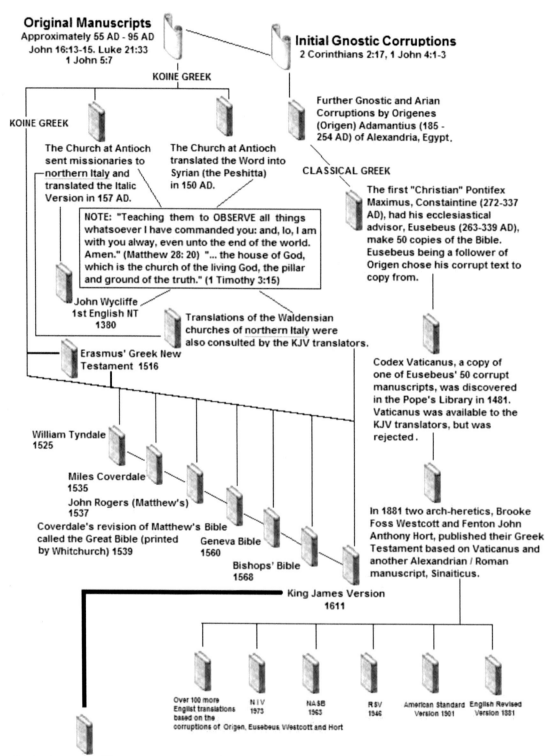

Why I Use the King James Bible

There are several reasons why I use the King James Bible. If you are new to the KJB, I hope that you will allow me to get you excited about putting out the extra effort it takes to get used to this Bible. Many people have urged me to use other versions of the bible such as the NKJV, ESV, NASB or NIV. I agree that it is possible for God to use these "easy to read" modern bible versions to save a soul. But God wants us also "to come unto the knowledge of the truth" (1 Tim. 2:4). Easier and popular is not always better.

I have come to understand that it is not only a matter of simply "taking out the thees and thous" but also that the changes in the modern bible versions are both textual and doctrinal. I hope you will realize that I have your best interest in mind and that I am only trying to bless you. After reading my reasons for using the King James Version of the Bible, I hope that you will understand its benefits and welcome the challenge. That you will apply yourself to enjoying it. Here are some of the reasons:

- The King James Bible cuts me to the heart and convicts my soul like no other Bible does. Try it for yourself, take any passage of Scripture and read it in various Bible translations, which one speaks to you?

- Although the original autographs no longer exist, God has preserved His word perfectly by exact copies of the originals. I believe that the KJB is the precise 100% accurate word of God. I believe God has kept His promise and preserved His word. I believe that He oversaw every step of the preservation of His word from the inspiration of Holy men moved by the Holy Spirit to write it, to the collection, translation (by 47 men who had the Holy Ghost in them), to the printing and publication.

- The Old Testament in the 1611 King James Bible is based on the Hebrew Masoretic Text, manuscripts carefully copied by hand by the Jewish scribes using strict rules to help prevent errors and departures from the original autographs. A small part of the Bible is in Aramaic, such as portions of the book of Daniel.

- In 1516 Erasmus published his collection of the best Greek New Testament manuscripts, called the Textus Receptus "received text." He gathered this from the Byzantines who fled to Europe after the Turks invaded what had been the Eastern Roman Empire in 1453. The King James New Testament, Martin Luther's German New Testament, and the Textus Receptus (King James Greek New Testament) are the only Bible versions which do not have any words of God omitted.

- **Over time and after a great deal of research I have come to understand that almost all modern bible versions are based on the corrupt Alexandrian texts, the Codex Vaticanus and the Codex Sinaiticus. These few texts have been eclectically (a little bit of this and a little bit of that) brought together into a "Critical Text" assembled (or concocted) by two unbelieving men, Westcott and Hort in 1881. Nestle-Aland/UBS (United Bible Society) also used the Westcott and Hort corrupt Greek New Testament. They included a Jesuit priest, Carlo Martini, on their Bible Committee. Higher Criticism, which swept over Germany and other parts of Europe after Martin Luther died, also denied the deity of Jesus.**

- For those new to the King James Bible it is valuable to know some of its features. The King James Bible is a word for word (formal equivalence) rather than a thought for thought (dynamic equivalence) translation. "Every word of God is pure" (Proverbs 30:5).

- **It is well worth it to get used to the pronouns used in the KJB because they are more specific than the general pronoun "you". If it has a "T" such as in "thee" and "thou" it is singular; if it has a "Y" as in "ye" it is plural. Thus: "I said unto thee (Nicodemus), Ye (plural you, meaning the nation of Israel) must be born again" (John 3:7).**

- **The KJB does not capitalize the pronoun names for God. To do so can be presumptive and it is left up to the reader to interpret the one referred to in the Bible with the help of the Holy Spirit. So please realize that although I capitalize words which pertain to God the KJB may have these words in lower case. Be prepared that British English in the KJB has a slightly different spelling than American English in words such as Saviour. In addition, the suffix "eth" indicates present tense such as "worketh."**

- The King James Bible (1611) does not use quotation marks, but capital letters begin a conversation. The spelling was updated in 1769.

- **The 47 King James Bible translators italicized words which they included for clarity but were not in the original manuscripts. Here is an example "I am *he*" (John 8:28). This lets the reader see at a glance what is written in the original word of God.**

- The cross references between the Old and the New Testament and other verses are easily accessed in the King James Bible. God's word is precise and concise. He uses similar words and phrases so we can compare them and understand more of His word. For more information, go to kjvtoday.com or get the excellent book *Bible Per-VERSIONS* by Eric and Lonna Neumann available on Amazon.

- The KJB uses the precise identical word or phrase for easy cross reference between the Old and the New Testament. For example, "the father of many nations" is found in Gen. 17:3, 4 and Rom. 4:17, 18. Furthermore, the KJB contains a unique number code.

- After the KJB was published in 1611 most people acquired this book rather than the very popular Geneva Bible because of its formal equivalence to the word of God and beautiful poetic language.

- Satan has been attacking God's word from the beginning "Yea, hath God said, Ye shall not eat of every tree of the garden?" (Gen. 3:1). But God has promised to preserve His word "The words of the LORD are pure words: as silver tried in a furnace of earth, purified seven times. Thou shalt keep them, O LORD, thou shalt preserve them from this generation for ever" (Psalms 12:6,7).

- God gave His Word through 40 different Jewish men over 1,500 years written in three different languages: Hebrew, Greek, and Aramaic. God preserved the Bible down through the centuries through dedicated copyists who meticulously copied it by hand. Yet this collection of 66 books fit together perfectly to reveal one continuous and complete blueprint of who God is, what He has done, and will do in heaven and on earth. This perfect continuity could only occur if God told these men what to write. The fulfilled prophecies confirm that God is the author.

The majority of all ancient Bible texts found, agree with the KJB. An excellent DVD documentary on how we got the King James Bible which includes Church history is *A Lamp in the Dark: The Untold History of the Bible* (A Chris Pinto Production) find it on Youtube or their website adullamfilms.com.

I used the NKJV for 15 years before I understood the problems with it. A good video on the NKJV problems on Youtube is the "New King James PerVersion." The New King James follows the Jehovah's Witness Bible in places calling Jesus a Servant instead of the Son of God. The subtle changes, omissions, and footnotes in the NKJV will not only weaken a person's faith, it takes a person away from the powerful true word of God found only in the King James Bible. Another excellent source for more information is Gail Riplinger "New Age Bible Versions" seminar on Youtube.com.

The NKJV does not use the same manuscript as the KJB. The NKJV uses the corrupt Stuttgart edition of the Old Testament Hebrew Text (ben Asher) not the Hebrew (ben Chayyim) used in the King James Bible. The NKJV omits the word "blood" 23 times; "Lord" 66 times; "God" 51 times; "heaven" 50 times; "repent" 44 times; "hell" 22 times; the following words are completely omitted "new testament, damnation, devils, JEHOVAH". The NKJV ignores the KJB Textus Receptus over 1,200 times. This information is taken from the website: Messiah Congregation oneinmessiah.net/njkv.htm.

Please notice how a very important verse for right division is changed in the New King James Version (NKJV) compare the following:

Rom. 15:8 (KJB) Now I say that Jesus Christ WAS a minister of the circumcision for the truth of God, to confirm the promises made unto the fathers.

Rom. 15:8 (NKJV) Now I say that Jesus Christ HAS BECOME a servant to the circumcision for the truth of God, to confirm the promises made to the fathers.

Christ <u>was</u> (NOT as the NKJV says: has become) a minister to the circumcision (Israel) when He was on earth, as Paul explained.

Here is an example of a doctrinal change in the New King James Version:

1 Cor. 1:18 (NKJV) For the message of the cross is foolishness to those who are perishing, but to us who are BEING SAVED it is the power of God.

1 Cor. 1:18 (KJB) For the preaching of the cross is to them that perish foolishness; but unto us which are SAVED it is the power of God.

Notice how the NKJV changed the doctrine of salvation to a progressive salvation, rather than a one-time instantaneous event saying we "are BEING SAVED" in 1 Cor. 1:18. No one can be secure if they are "being saved," instead of "are saved." The NKJV is a counterfeit bible, <u>not</u> the KJV.

God's Secret

The New International Version (NIV) is missing 17 entire verses. Try finding Acts 8:37 in the NIV. Here is the list of missing verses (some newer NIV bibles have these verses in the footnotes, but they belong in the text):

Matthew 17:21; 18:11; 23:14.

Mark 7:16; 9:44; 9:46; 11:26; 15:28.

Luke 17:36; 23:17; John 5:4.

Acts 8:37; 15:34; 24:7; 28:29.

Romans 16:24 and 1 John 5:7.

Philo (25 BC–50 AD), a Jewish man, tried to unite Greek philosophy (Plato) with the Jewish Old Testament. Origen (185-254 AD) did much damage to God's word by changing it in Alexandria, Egypt. The true line of Bibles came from the Antioch line. Paul says that "after my departing shall grievous wolves enter in among you, not sparing the flock. Also of your own selves shall men arise, speaking perverse things" (Acts 20:29, 30a). Paul also writes "For we are not as many which corrupt the word of God" (2 Cor. 2:17). See if this verse is quoted correctly in your Bible "God was manifest in the flesh" (1 Tim. 3:16) (some bibles leave out "God"). Satan is taking the true word of God away from Christians and many are unaware of what is happening.

The KJB translators primarily used the Greek texts of Stephanus 1550 and Beza 1598. I believe the King James Bible is the true word of God in the English language, perfectly based on the true Greek and Hebrew texts which God has preserved. There are really only two Bibles in the world today those based on God's preserved texts like the KJB, and all the others based on corrupt texts. "How firm a foundation He has laid for us all in His excellent word." We need to use the most accurate text in our Bible study. For all these reasons I believe that I would be wasting your time and mine if I use any other Bible version.

God does not want His word changed in any way, NOT added or subtracted to: "... If any man shall add unto these things, God shall add unto him the plagues that are written in this book: And if any man shall take away from the words of the book of this prophecy, God shall take away his part out of the book of life, and out of the holy city, and from the things which are written in this book" (Rev. 22:18,19).

A Primer with Pictures for How to Rightly Divide the Word of Truth

Satan used the Catholic church to keep the Bible from the common people. The false Alexandrian text (the Vulgate) was kept in a dead language which few could read (Latin) shut up for the 1,000-year Dark Ages (500-1500 AD). But Martin Luther hatched the egg that Erasmus had laid by translating the Textus Receptus which Erasmus had collected so that people could read it.

William Tyndale (1494-1536) was the first to translate the Greek (TR) and Hebrew Bible into English. It has been estimated that as much as 90 percent of the King James Bible was the work of Tyndale (Bere, Michael *Bible Doctrines for Today*, A Beka Book, Pensacola, FL 1996, page 79).

Remember, the modern bible versions hide (obscure) the revelation of the "mystery" given to Paul. But the mystery is evident in the King James Bible for those who study the Bible rightly divided.

Proving the superiority of the King James Bible is simple and easy: the KJV exalts the Lord Jesus Christ more than any other Bible on the planet. The true scriptures testify of Jesus Christ and exalt Him.

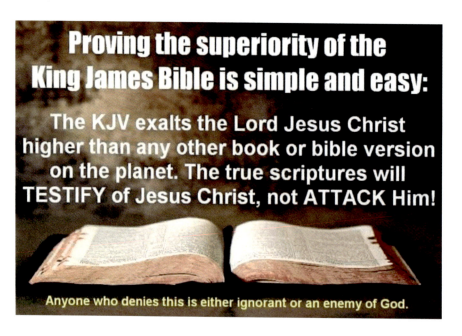

The KJB (also known as the KJV) is a masterpiece inspired and preserved by God the Holy Spirit. The Lord Jesus Christ, the Word (John 1:1-4) said that His words are eternal "heaven and earth shall pass away, but MY WORDS SHALL NOT PASS AWAY" (Matt. 24:35).

Now I not only use the King James Bible, but believe it is God's perfect word.

God's Secret

Paul's followers preserved the true word of God in Antioch.

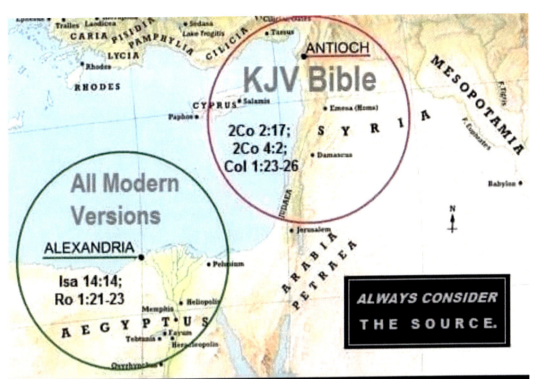

A Primer with Pictures for How to Rightly Divide the Word of Truth

The Faith of Jesus

I was stunned by how many different times the King James Bible states that we are saved by the "faith of Jesus"; "faith of Christ"; "his faith"; "the faith that is in me" and so on. I had always been told that salvation depended on our own faith. I began to investigate this observation on a deeper level.

I found that very few pastors teach on the "Doctrine of the Faith of Jesus Christ" or even know about it. There are nearly a dozen verses in the King James Bible that refer to this little-known doctrine.

When Jesus commissioned Paul on the road to Damascus He said it was His faith that would save the Gentiles. Jesus said, ". . . the Gentiles, unto whom now I send thee, to open their eyes, and to turn them from darkness to light, and from the power of Satan unto God, that they may receive forgiveness of sins, and inheritance among them which are sanctified by <u>faith that is in me</u>" (Acts 26:17, 18).

Notice that the following verse refers to the faith of Jesus twice with the faith of the believer sandwiched in the middle: "Knowing that a man is not justified by the works of the law, but by the <u>faith of Jesus Christ, even we have believed in Jesus Christ</u>, that we might be justified by the <u>faith of Jesus Christ</u>, and not by the works of the law: for by the works of the law shall no flesh be justified" (Gal. 2:16).

<u>We are justified because of the faith of Jesus</u> and by our faith in Him and what He has done. Notice the many verses that mention the faith "of" Jesus:

"I am crucified with Christ: nevertheless I live; yet not I, but Christ liveth in me: and the life which I now live in the flesh I live by the <u>faith of the Son of God</u>, who loved me, and gave himself for me" (Gal. 2:20).

"But the scripture hath concluded all under sin, that the promise by <u>faith of Jesus Christ</u> might be given to them that believe" (Gal. 3:22).

We can trust the faith of Jesus. "According to the eternal purpose which he purposed in Christ Jesus our Lord: In whom we have boldness and access with confidence <u>by the faith of him</u>" (Eph. 3:11, 12).

We put our faith "in" the Lord Jesus Christ and we are "in Him," by faith in His faith. Put no confidence in the flesh, but only in what Jesus has done.

God's Secret

All modern bibles omit the little word "of" in the phrase "faith of Jesus" and substitute the word "in" disguising the doctrine of the FAITH OF JESUS.

Why is the doctrine of the faith of Jesus absent from all modern bibles? Because Satan hates this doctrine. We may not fully comprehend the magnitude of this doctrine this side of eternity.

Jesus obeyed His Father perfectly even to the point of death on the cross. Jesus prayed to His Father often, talking with Him and receiving instruction.

Jesus mentioned His dependence on the Father while here on earth. "The Son can do nothing of himself, but what he seeth the Father do" (John 5:19), and "I can of mine own self do nothing . . . I seek not mine own will, but the will of the Father" (John 5:30). Jesus had to trust in the Father's plan of redemption.

On earth, Jesus was instructed by the word of God. He said, "It is written, That man shall not live by bread alone, but by every word of God" (Luke 4:4).

As the God-Man, Jesus was fully God and He was also fully Man. Jesus Christ did not cease to be God. But He humbled Himself and took on the form of a servant "the Word [Jesus] was made flesh [human], and dwelt among us" (John 1:14). Jesus willingly laid aside His privileges as God (the independent use of His attributes) and became dependent on the Father. "Who, being in the form of God [100% God], thought it not robbery to be equal with God: But made himself of no reputation, and took upon him the form of a servant, and was made in the likeness of men [100% Man]: And being found in fashion as a man, he humbled himself, and became obedient unto death, even the death of the cross" (Phil. 2:6-8).

The temptation not to go to the cross was so strong that Jesus overcame it by sweating "as it were great drops of blood" (Luke 22:44). Jesus told His Father "not my will, but thine, be done" (Luke 22:42) demonstrating His faith in the Father's plan for Him to go to the cross.

Not for one second did Jesus ever lose His faith; because if He had Jesus would have had to die for His own sins and could not have died for ours.

Jesus put His faith in the Father depending on Him perfectly while finishing all that needed to be done to save us. Salvation is 100% what God has done, and 0% what we have done.

Faith and love are in the Lord Jesus Christ. His faith never wavered because of His love for us, "And the grace of our Lord was exceeding abundant with faith and love which is in Christ Jesus" (1 Tim. 1:14).

We put our faith in the faith of Jesus by believing God's word "the holy scriptures which are able to make thee wise unto salvation through faith which is in Christ Jesus" (2 Tim. 3:15).

About 2,000 years ago Jesus, the Son of God, had the faith to shed His own blood to purchase our redemption. He finished paying for all the sins of all people that ever lived so that those who believe in Him will be His spiritually alive children forever. Because of the perfect faith of Jesus, we can confidently put our faith in Him.

The Lord Jesus Christ had perfect faith in the Father in order to accomplish His work on the cross. The Father was satisfied with His blood atonement and raised Him from the dead. "He . . . shall be satisfied" (Isaiah 53:11).

Salvation is a gift given to a sinner, who has become a child of God, by grace through faith. Christ's righteousness is imputed to us when we believe that He died for our sins. Christ paid for our sins and gave us His righteousness.

The merit is in the faith of Jesus Christ by whom we receive righteousness. "Even the righteousness of God which is by <u>faith of Jesus Christ</u> unto all and upon all them that believe: for there is no difference" (Romans 3:22).

"And be found in him, not having our own righteousness, which is of the law, but that which is through the <u>faith of Christ</u>, the righteousness which is of God by faith" (Phil. 3:9).

We just believe. It was the "<u>faith of Jesus</u>" that accomplished the cross, and we just need to have faith in what He has done. Jesus had the faith to complete the mission the Father gave Him to do. We put our faith in His faith.

If the "faith of Jesus" is replaced with our "faith in Jesus" then the emphasis is no longer on Jesus but on the believer.

The little word "of" can make a big difference.

God's Secret

Right Division Produces Peace of Mind

The pure grace message for us in the body of Christ is found in Paul's letters. We have grace and peace in this dispensation. When we apply the "sound doctrine" found in Paul's letters we are free and stable. But if we apply Christ's earthly ministry to ourselves we have doubt, legalism, and confusion. Once you have come to the knowledge of the truth share it with someone else. A conversation starter could be "do you ever wonder about life after death?" or, "do you know that God had a <u>secret</u> before the foundation of the world?"

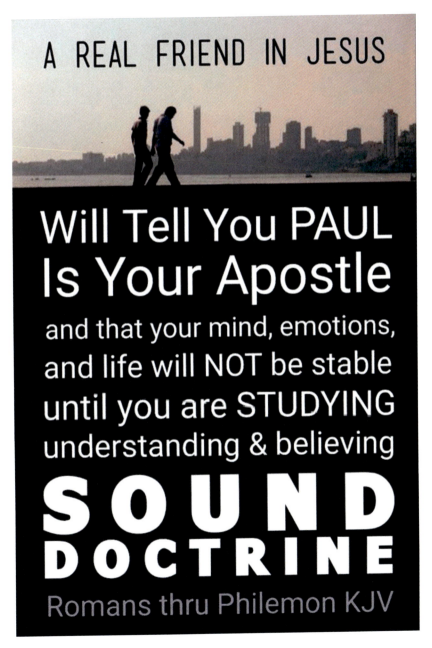

A Primer with Pictures for How to Rightly Divide the Word of Truth

About the Author

I used to believe that there was no God; that the only one I could count on was myself. I didn't know I was lost. Then when I was an adult, my father told me he believed there is a higher being. That opened my mind to God a sliver. In nurse-midwife school, I learned that I had to take care of the "whole" patient. I wondered how I could help them spiritually. I asked some Christian girls who lived above me in the apartment building to teach me about the Bible.

After several lessons, I understood the Bible was unlike any other book: it was the word of God. A few weeks later I understood that Jesus Christ died for my sins, was buried and rose again. I was translated out of Adam into Christ that very second. From that very moment, I was "complete in Christ" (Col. 2:10). I thank God for saving me so soundly in 1990. Later I came to understand that the Church of Christ was a cult, but that is another story.

Fortunately, I didn't stay in that church long. Soon I moved to San Diego and went to a non-denominational Christian church. I found out that salvation is by grace "through faith" (Eph. 2:8). This church had expository Bible teaching with charismatic leanings and was Acts 2 (mixers). Personally, I never had any of the spiritual gifts some in that church claimed to have.

In 2014 I came to understand that the King James Bible was the true word of God. I tried to tell others in several churches this but they rejected that truth, and me. Consequently, I made many new friendships with like-minded people.

God's Secret

In the spring of 2015, while trying to understand when the Rapture would occur, I began watching Les Feldick teach the Bible on Youtube. That is how I came to understand the importance of Paul's ministry and the difference between law and grace. I also learned that there is a distinction between what was preached to Israel and the earthly kingdom believers (law), and the body of Christ believers bound for the heavenly places (grace).

I realized that the body of Christ believers in the dispensation of grace will reign with Christ in the heavenly places. This is the SECRET! <u>The present dispensation of grace is a giant parenthesis between the two appearances of the Lord Jesus Christ in the air (one to Paul, and next the rapture). The body of Christ has been forming for nearly 2,000 years and will soon be taken out.</u>

All of the Bible is "for us" but "not to us, nor about us." (Most of the Bible is to Israel, and only Paul's 13 letters are directly to us).

Our Lord Jesus Christ won the victory at Calvary. He is in the process of reclaiming both heaven and earth from Satan and populating both realms with true believers. I discovered that this belief is known as Mid Acts 9 Dispensationalism.

It is now 2017. A year ago, I found my way to a church that believes as I do. I am very content and excited. This church was also willing to send elders to teach a small Bible Study in my home in San Diego. It is such a privilege to host the study; I am so blessed.

Let us spur each other on to do mighty things for His Majesty! Let us do our part to reconcile others to Christ, and "to make all men see what *is* the fellowship of the mystery, which from the beginning of the world hath been hid in God who created all things by Jesus Christ" (Eph. 3:9).

*Final note: Paul told Timothy to "give attendance to reading" (1 Tim. 4:13). The most important book to read daily is the <u>King James Bible</u>. We must cultivate a love for His word, that we might know Him, His plan and purpose.

The best books to read in the Bible are Romans to Philemon.

<u>Begin with reading Romans to establish yourself in the faith</u>. Then read the other letters of Paul which complete the "sound doctrine" for the body of Christ. Paul begins each one of his letters with his name. At the judgment seat of Christ, we will be judged on our service done while in "his body." Building on <u>sound doctrine</u> is important. Remember Paul said, "Consider what I [Paul] say; and the Lord give thee understanding in all things" (2 Tim. 2:7).

A Primer with Pictures for How to Rightly Divide the Word of Truth

Other books by Marianne Manley available on Amazon.com

Could God Have a 7,000 Year Plan for Mankind?

AD 34 The Year Jesus Died for All (same content as *Could God*, in 9x6 size)

Treasure Hunt is the name of the book that she is currently working on.

As a retired Nurse Midwife, Marianne Manley has also written:

Birth Stories and Midwife Notes: In God We Trust

Born at Home, Praise the Lord!

Handbook for Christian Natural Childbirth

Christian Childbirth

A Mother's Loving Instruction to Her Daughter

To contact the author, go to:

www.Acts9GraceBibleChurch.com

www.Christianmidwife.com

Find her on Facebook at facebook.com/marianne.manley.7

The author may be contacted by e-mail at mariannemanley@sbcglobal.net

Made in the USA
Lexington, KY
21 April 2018